Symbiotic Horizons

THIRD EDITION

SYMBIOTIC HORIZONS

Exploring the AI-Human Connection

CAN BARTU H.

2024

Symbiotic Horizons

Can Bartu H.

Foreword

Welcome to an insightful journey into the evolving landscape of artificial intelligence and its profound impact on our world. This book invites you to explore the intricate relationship between technological advancement and human experience.

In an era where innovation rapidly reshapes the fabric of our daily lives, AI stands at the forefront, challenging our perceptions and presenting boundless opportunities. This volume delves deeply into the complex interplay between AI and humanity, examining the promises it holds, the challenges it presents, and the crucial ethical considerations that must guide its development.

As you navigate these pages, you will discover the remarkable potential of AI to revolutionize fields such as healthcare, education, business, and creative endeavors. The ability of AI to augment human capabilities and unlock new frontiers of knowledge will undoubtedly inspire awe at the possibilities that lie ahead.

However, this exploration is not solely focused on optimism. It also embraces the vital responsibility that accompanies AI's rapid growth. Critical questions are raised regarding ethical AI development, human-AI collaboration, and the necessity of maintaining a human-centric perspective in an AI-driven world. By examining the complex challenges and risks, the authors endeavor to pave the way for a harmonious coexistence with AI.

Each chapter has been meticulously crafted to provide a comprehensive understanding of AI's multifaceted nature. As you read, you will find yourself engrossed in the dynamic interaction between technology and humanity, exploring how AI can empower us while upholding our values and societal well-being. We encourage you to embark on this intellectual adventure, to challenge your perspectives, and to reflect on the future we are collectively shaping.

May this exploration ignite your curiosity, awaken your imagination, and empower you to navigate the future with knowledge and compassion. Happy reading!

CONTENTS

CHAPTER 1

Introduction

1.1 The Connection Between Artificial Intelligence and Humanity

The dating among Artificial Intelligence (AI) and humanity is a subject of extraordinary importance and complexity. As AI generation advances at a fast pace, its integration into numerous elements of our lives raises profound questions about our destiny interplay and coexistence with this transformative pressure.

AI's journey dates returned to the early endeavors of pc scientists who aimed to mimic human intelligence in machines. Over the years, AI has advanced and matured, attaining milestones in fields like tool studying, natural language processing, laptop imaginative and prescient, and robotics. These advancements have contributed to the large adoption of AI across industries and have brought about AI turning into an inseparable a part of modern life.

One of the essential aspects of the connection between AI and humanity lies inside the augmentation of human abilities. AI technologies, particularly machine learning algorithms and neural networks, have established their prowess in processing huge quantities of facts and performing complex obligations with unheard of speed and accuracy. This augmentation of human abilties holds giant potential to revolutionize severa sectors, starting from healthcare and finance to production and transportation.

In our daily lives, AI has turn out to be an increasing number of integrated and pervasive. Virtual assistants, chatbots, and clever devices have end up commonplace, streamlining numerous responsibilities and presenting customized studies. AI-powered advice structures have transformed how we devour content and make buying choices. Moreover, AI's function in industries like healthcare has added approximately advanced diagnosis accuracy and extra effective remedy plans.

However, this integration of AI into society additionally increases ethical issues. The deployment of AI algorithms in preference-making strategies, along side hiring, lending, and crook justice, has sparked worries about bias and fairness. Additionally, the difficulty of statistics privacy and protection is a tremendous issue, as AI structures depend upon extensive amounts of statistics for training and optimization.

Furthermore, the concern of system displacement because of AI automation has turn out to be a normal project. While AI has the functionality to optimize workflows and decorate productivity, it has additionally added approximately anxieties about the future of hard work and the want for reskilling and upskilling the personnel.

AI's impact on creativity and the humanities has also been a topic of exploration. AI-generated artwork, tune, and literature have sparked debates about the essence of human creativity and the placement of AI in ingenious expression.

While AI can produce super works, the query of whether it possesses real creativity and emotion remains open to interpretation.

Addressing the ethical implications of AI and ensuring accountable AI development are essential steps in fostering a harmonious relationship amongst synthetic intelligence and humanity. Stakeholders, which include governments, agencies, researchers, and the general public, want to collaboratively work to set up robust AI governance frameworks that promote transparency, equity, and obligation.

The connection between artificial intelligence and humanity is complicated and multifaceted. AI's transformative potential offers numerous possibilities for societal improvement, financial increase, and clinical discovery. However, to navigate this new era successfully, it's miles critical to address moral traumatic situations and format AI structures that align with human values and aspirations. By doing so, we're capable of foster a destiny wherein AI and humanity coexist symbiotically, bringing about notable advancements for the betterment of our worldwide community.

1.2 Purpose and Structure of the Book

The reason of this e book is to discover the problematic courting amongst Artificial Intelligence (AI) and humanity, focusing on the possibilities, traumatic situations, and ability implications that rise up from their interaction. As AI continues to revolutionize severa domain names of our lives, facts its effect on humanity and society turns into paramount.

The ebook goals to offer a complete and balanced evaluation of the multifaceted connection among AI and humanity. By delving into diverse aspects of this dating, we trying to find to offer readers a nuanced angle that is going past the floor-degree discussions on AI.

In the introductory section, we set the level for the exploration thru providing a pinnacle degree view of the rise of AI, from its origins to the modern-day state of the sector. This historical context permits readers draw near the transformative adventure of AI and its implications for the destiny.

Chapter 1 specializes in the enhancement of human skills through AI. We delve into the techniques AI technology augment human choice-making, problem-fixing, and creative capabilities. Understanding how AI empowers people and companies is vital in appreciating its capacity benefits for society.

Chapter 2 explores AI's integration into our day by day lives. We have a take a look at actual-world programs of AI, including virtual assistants, recommendation structures, and self sufficient vehicles, to reveal off how AI influences diverse industries and sectors. Through these examples, readers advantage insights into the practical implications of AI on a global scale.

Ethical worries take center diploma in Chapter 3. We deal with troubles related to bias in AI algorithms, facts privacy, and transparency. Analyzing the moral stressful situations surrounding AI is important in fostering responsible AI development and ensuring AI aligns with human values and societal norms.

Chapter 4 delves into the priority of activity displacement due to AI automation. We speak the ability impact of AI at the workforce, the want for reskilling, and the importance of making geared up for the destiny technique panorama. Navigating the changes brought by means of using AI inside the hard work market calls for a proactive technique to assist the body of people.

AI's characteristic in creativity and the arts is the focus of Chapter 5. By studying AI-generated artwork, music, and literature, we find out the bounds of AI's modern competencies and its courting with human creativity. Understanding this interplay enriches the discourse on the position of AI in shaping cultural expression.

In Chapter 6, we talk the look for ethical AI and the role of various stakeholders in selling fairness, transparency, and duty in AI systems. Building ethical AI is a collective obligation that necessitates collaboration among governments, groups, and researchers.

In the conclusion, we summarize the important thing findings and insights from the e-book. We reiterate the significance of AI's effect on humanity and underscore the importance of ethical issues in shaping the destiny of AI.

The reason and form of this ebook intention to provide readers a comprehensive understanding of the relationship between AI and humanity. By inspecting AI's potential, demanding situations, and ethical implications, we are hoping to foster informed discussions and preference-making that pave the way for a harmonious coexistence between AI and humanity, making sure that AI serves as a pressure for first rate development and human advancement.

CHAPTER 2

The History and Development of Artificial Intelligence

2.1 Origins and Early Steps of Artificial Intelligence

2.1.1 Alan Turing and the Turing Test

Alan Turing, a pioneering mathematician, fact seeker, and pc scientist, performed a pivotal position within the improvement of modern computing and artificial intelligence. Born in 1912, Turing's contributions to the fields of arithmetic and pc era are celebrated to these days. Among his many groundbreaking thoughts, the idea of the Turing Test stands as a widespread milestone in the check of AI.

The Turing Test, proposed by using Alan Turing in his 1950 paper titled "Computing Machinery and Intelligence," sought to cope with the question of whether or not machines have to show off human-like intelligence. Turing expected a take a look at wherein a human evaluator engages in herbal language conversations with each a human and a device, with out information that is which. If the evaluator cannot reliably distinguish the various human and the device based on their responses, the device is said to have handed the Turing Test and installed artificial intelligence.

The Turing Test laid the inspiration for the observe of tool intelligence and the search for growing wondering machines. Turing's interest on conversation and language as a defining factor of intelligence turned into innovative at the time and remains influential within the AI area nowadays.

Although the Turing Test became a landmark concept, it has moreover sparked debates and evaluations. Some argue that the capability to pass the Turing Test is merely a measure of superficial human-like conduct, not always indicative of genuine intelligence or interest. Others query the check's capacity to seize all elements of human intelligence, which encompasses feelings, creativity, and self-consciousness, attributes that machines might not own.

Nevertheless, Turing's contributions to the improvement of AI extended past the Turing Test. During World War II, Turing performed a important feature in breaking the German Enigma code, extensively contributing to the Allied victory. His paintings on the theoretical foundations of computation, referred to as the Turing gadget, laid the basis for current computer systems and computation concept.

Tragically, Turing's lifestyles have become reduce brief on the age of 41. In 1952, he changed into prosecuted for his homosexuality, which modified into then criminalized in the United Kingdom. As a end result, Turing endured chemical castration as an opportunity to imprisonment. He tragically died years later, in 1954.

In recognition of his pioneering contributions, Turing is notably regarded as one of the fathers of cutting-edge computing and synthetic intelligence. His legacy keeps to encourage researchers and practitioners of their pursuit of statistics and developing AI. The Turing Test, even as no longer a definitive degree of AI, remains an important historic milestone and a notion-scary concept within the ongoing exploration of gadget intelligence and its courting with human intelligence. Turing's effect at the fields of AI and computing is immeasurable, and his paintings keeps to shape the trajectory of technology and human know-how to this modern.

2.1.2 Fundamental Concepts of Artificial Intelligence

Artificial Intelligence (AI) is a multidisciplinary area that interests to create clever machines able to performing responsibilities that normally require human intelligence. The development of AI is primarily based mostly on numerous critical ideas that underpin its functioning and packages.

Machine studying is a important thing of AI that lets in machines to have a look at from data and decorate their normal performance through the years without being explicitly programmed. By using diverse algorithms and statistical techniques, machines can perceive patterns, make predictions, and adapt their conduct based mostly on the facts they get preserve of. Supervised, unsupervised, and reinforcement studying are common sorts of machine getting to know strategies used to teach AI fashions.

Inspired thru the human mind's shape and functioning, neural networks are a critical idea in AI. They are interconnected layers of synthetic neurons that method statistics and take a look at from facts. Neural networks are on the middle of deep studying, a subset of machine reading that has completed incredible success in duties together with photo popularity, herbal language processing, and playing video games.

NLP makes a speciality of permitting machines to understand, interpret, and generate human language. It includes duties together with speech popularity, language translation, sentiment assessment, and chatbots. NLP strategies permit machines to engage with humans in a extra herbal and intuitive way, beginning up a big variety of programs in verbal exchange and information processing.

Computer vision is the field of AI that empowers machines to interpret and understand visual information from the arena. By the usage of photo and video processing strategies, AI structures can take a look at and recognize devices, faces, and scenes, permitting programs which encompass facial popularity, impartial vehicles, and clinical imaging.

Knowledge example involves encoding data and information in a layout that AI systems can apprehend and manipulate. It allows AI fashions to cause and make choices based totally on the available know-how. Different information instance techniques, consisting of semantic networks, ontologies, and information graphs, are used to organize and way facts effectively.

AI systems use algorithms and heuristics to plan and make choices in complex environments. By comparing viable movements and their consequences, AI fashions can decide the maximum simplest path of movement to attain a selected aim. Planning and desire-making skills are critical in numerous AI programs, together with robotics, self sustaining systems, and strategic video games.

Robotics is an interdisciplinary vicinity that combines AI, engineering, and mechanics to format and construct wise machines, called robots. AI-powered robots may have interaction with the bodily international, understand their surroundings, and perform duties autonomously. They discover programs in industries which includes production, healthcare, exploration, and seek and rescue operations.

These fundamental principles shape the spine of synthetic intelligence, allowing machines to simulate human-like intelligence and behavior. The ongoing improvements in AI studies and technology hold to increase the limits of what AI systems can gain, beginning up new opportunities and traumatic situations for the duration of numerous domains. As AI evolves, the ones center principles continue to be important in shaping the destiny of clever machines and their integration into our day by day lives.

2.2 The Development and Milestones of Artificial Intelligence

2.2.1 Early Artificial Intelligence Programs and Applications

The origins of synthetic intelligence can be traced again to the pioneering efforts of laptop scientists and researchers who sought to create machines that would mimic human intelligence.

Developed with the useful resource of Allen Newell and Herbert A. Simon in 1955, Logic Theorist was one of the earliest AI applications. It aimed to show mathematical theorems using standards of desirable judgment and heuristic seek. Logic Theorist established that machines can also want to reflect human-like hassle-fixing capabilities and paved the manner for destiny work in automatic reasoning and theorem proving.

Also created by way of Allen Newell and Herbert A. Simon, GPS, introduced in 1957, was an influential AI application designed to clear up a sizeable range of issues. It used a problem-solving approach based totally mostly on technique-ends analysis and could adapt its hassle-solving strategies based on in advance enjoy. GPS represented a sizable step closer to developing more flexible and adaptive AI structures.

Often taken into consideration the beginning of AI as a region, the Dartmouth workshop took place inside the summer time of 1956. Led through John McCarthy, Marvin Minsky, Nathaniel Rochester, and Claude Shannon, the workshop brought collectively distinguished researchers to talk about the possibility of making "wondering machines" and coined the term "synthetic intelligence." This occasion marked the beginning of organized AI studies and catalyzed enhancements in AI technology.

Developed through Joseph Weizenbaum in 1966, ELIZA become a natural language processing application that simulated communication with a human psychotherapist. ELIZA used pattern matching and clean language policies to interact clients in text-based totally interactions. Although especially number one, ELIZA tested how AI might also need to create the phantasm of expertise and empathy via language interactions.

Created inside the past due 1960s at the Stanford Research Institute, Shakey changed into one of the first mobile robots able to autonomous navigation and manipulation. Shakey used a mixture of cameras, sensors, and AI algorithms to map its surroundings and plan its moves. It became a pioneering instance of AI packages in robotics and laid the basis for future tendencies in autonomous systems.

Developed in the early 1970s, MYCIN modified into an expert tool designed to help in scientific analysis and treatment hints for bacterial infections. It used a rule-based totally technique and a expertise base of medical facts to provide personalized guidelines based totally on affected man or woman symptoms and scientific history. MYCIN showcased the capability of AI in specialised domains and highlighted the advantages of mixing human knowledge with AI talents.

These early AI programs and programs marked vast milestones inside the region's history, demonstrating the ability of machines to simulate human-like intelligence and hassle-fixing competencies. Although the ones packages may appear simplistic compared to modern-day AI structures, they laid the inspiration for the evolution of AI era and set the degree for the transformative upgrades witnessed in present day AI applications. The lessons located out from these early endeavors maintain to persuade AI research and development, shaping the trajectory of the field because it progresses into new frontiers of artificial intelligence.

2.2.2 The Rise and Impact of Deep Learning

Deep Learning has emerged as one of the maximum revolutionary and influential advancements inside the field of Artificial Intelligence (AI). It has notably converted various industries and programs, pushing the boundaries of what AI can reap.

Deep studying is a subset of device mastering that makes a speciality of training synthetic neural networks with more than one layers, additionally referred to as deep neural networks. These networks can robotically learn to constitute and extract hierarchical styles and competencies from complex statistics, making them specially effective in responsibilities regarding photograph popularity, herbal language processing, and other regions.

The concept of deep neural networks dates again to the Forties with the development of the primary synthetic neurons and perceptrons. However, it wasn't until the 1980s and 1990s that researchers began experimenting with deeper architectures, dealing with large disturbing conditions in schooling such networks effectively.

The development of the backpropagation set of guidelines within the 1980s modified right into a important milestone for deep learning. Backpropagation enabled green training of deep neural networks through calculating gradients and updating the community's parameters all through the studying system. This breakthrough allowed researchers to build deeper networks and significantly progressed their ordinary overall performance.

Convolutional Neural Networks, brought within the 1990s and popularized inside the early 2010s, revolutionized laptop imaginative and prescient obligations. CNNs leverage convolutional layers to routinely take a look at hierarchical representations from picture data, permitting accurate picture recognition, item detection, and image technology.

In the mid-2010s, deep gaining knowledge of started out making giant contributions to NLP obligations. Recurrent Neural Networks (RNNs) and Long Short-Term Memory (LSTM) networks enabled the improvement of language models able to processing sequential statistics, main to breakthroughs in machine translation, sentiment evaluation, and chatbots.

Deep mastering additionally made massive strides in reinforcement studying, a branch of AI centered on schooling sellers to analyze from their interactions with an environment. Deep Reinforcement Learning algorithms, in conjunction with Deep Q Networks (DQNs) and Proximal Policy Optimization (PPO), have carried out first rate success in complex obligations, such as undertaking gambling, robotics, and self reliant systems.

The upward thrust of deep getting to know has had a profound impact on numerous industries and packages. In healthcare, deep gaining knowledge of aids in medical imaging assessment, disease diagnosis, and drug discovery. In finance, it contributes to fraud detection and algorithmic buying and selling. In unbiased vehicles, deep gaining knowledge of permits superior notion and choice-making talents. Deep getting to know has additionally revolutionized the enjoyment industry, with AI-generated content material cloth and advice systems shaping character reviews.

Deep studying's fulfillment may be attributed in element to enhancements in hardware, especially Graphics Processing Units (GPUs) and specialized AI chips. These technology drastically accelerate the education and inference of deep neural networks, making big-scale deep studying models feasible.

The upward thrust of deep studying has essentially converted AI studies and programs. Its success in complicated responsibilities and its potential to leverage big quantities of records have driven improvements across various domains. As deep mastering maintains to bolster, it holds the promise of unlocking new frontiers in AI and contributing to solving some of the most urgent demanding situations going thru society. As a using force in the AI revolution, deep mastering maintains to shape the future of generation, impacting industries and our each day lives in splendid methods.

2.3 Current Artificial Intelligence Technologies and Applications

2.3.1 Self-Driving Cars and Autonomous Systems

Self-using automobiles and autonomous systems constitute a transformative utility of synthetic intelligence and robotics. These era reason to revolutionize transportation via permitting motors and machines to function without human intervention.

The concept of self-driving automobiles dates returned numerous many years, however sizable progress has been made in brand new years. Advances in sensor technology, gadget gaining knowledge of, and computer imaginative and prescient have been instrumental in growing independent automobiles capable of navigating actual-worldwide environments.

Self-using cars and unique autonomous systems depend upon a aggregate of sensors, AI algorithms, and control systems. Lidar, radar, cameras, and ultrasonic sensors provide real-time records approximately the automobile's surroundings, even as AI algorithms procedure this statistics to make using selections. Control systems translate those alternatives into specific actions, allowing the vehicle to navigate correctly.

The Society of Automotive Engineers (SAE) has defined six stages of using automation, starting from Level 0 (no automation) to Level 5 (complete automation). Level 2 and Level 3 systems provide confined motive force assistance, at the same time as Level 4 and Level 5 constitute high and whole automation, respectively, with minimum or no human intervention required.

Safety is a paramount difficulty in the improvement of self-driving automobiles. Autonomous systems have to meet rigorous safety necessities and go through considerable sorting out earlier than deployment on public roads. Governments and regulatory bodies play a essential function in defining the criminal framework for self reliant vehicles and making sure public safety.

Self-the usage of motors have the potential to enhance avenue safety with the resource of reducing human error, that is a main purpose of injuries. They can also decorate web page site visitors performance, reduce congestion, and provide mobility answers for aged or disabled individuals who may have constrained get right of entry to to transportation.

Despite huge progress, self-driving motors face numerous traumatic situations and obstacles. Adapting to unpredictable human behavior, damaging weather conditions, and complex city environments stays a formidable venture. Ethical concerns, collectively with the trolley hassle (a ethical capture 22 situation in which the car should make selections that may damage its passengers or pedestrians), moreover gift moral demanding situations.

Public belief and popularity of self-driving automobiles are important for his or her large adoption. Building public accept as real with requires obvious communication approximately the talents and barriers of self reliant systems, further to addressing concerns related to protection, privateness, and ability task displacement.

The concept of autonomy extends beyond self-riding cars to extraordinary domains. Autonomous drones are being used in numerous industries, which include agriculture, surveillance, and transport services. Additionally, independent robots are hired in manufacturing, warehouses, and healthcare settings, streamlining operations and augmenting human skills.

The tremendous adoption of self-using motors and autonomous structures could reshape cities and transportation infrastructure. It may result in decreased car possession, modifications in metropolis making plans, and new company fashions inside the transportation enterprise.

Self-driving automobiles and unbiased structures constitute a transformative utility of AI and robotics. While widespread progress has been made, the adventure toward certainly self sustaining automobiles and systems keeps. Addressing technical, regulatory, and ethical traumatic situations is critical to unlocking the entire capacity of autonomous technology, ushering in a brand new era of transportation and automation with the capability to beautify protection, performance, and accessibility.

2.3.2 Natural Language Processing and Speech Recognition

Natural Language Processing (NLP) and Speech Recognition are interconnected branches of Artificial Intelligence (AI) that focus on permitting machines to recognize, interpret, and engage with human language in a natural and meaningful way.

NLP is a subject of AI that desires to bridge the distance amongst human language and device understanding. Its primary purpose is to permit machines to recognise, technique, and generate human language in written or spoken forms. NLP era have a wide variety of programs and characteristic come to be an vital a part of our daily lives.

Tokenization: Tokenization consists of breaking down a text into smaller gadgets, collectively with words or terms, to investigate and manner the language correctly.

NLP systems assign grammatical tags to terms, identifying their roles as nouns, verbs, adjectives, and plenty of others., to recognize sentence structure.

NER identifies and categorizes entities like names of human beings, companies, locations, and dates in a textual content.

NLP algorithms can have a look at and decide the sentiment or emotion expressed in a piece of text, whether or not or not effective, bad, or impartial.

NLP is used to build language translation systems like Google Translate, facilitating communication throughout super languages.

NLP lets in the development of conversational AI entrepreneurs that interact with clients thru natural language interfaces.

Search engines rent NLP to understand patron queries and retrieve applicable information from big databases.

NLP algorithms can robotically generate concise summaries of prolonged texts.

Speech reputation, additionally referred to as Automatic Speech Recognition (ASR), is a subset of NLP focused on changing spoken language into written text. The generation allows machines to recognize and transcribe human speech correctly.

Acoustic fashions study audio signals to pick out out phonemes and map them to phrases and phrases.

Language fashions use probability distributions to are awaiting the most probable collection of terms primarily based at the context.

The combination of acoustic and language fashions lets in speech reputation systems to convert spoken terms into written text.

Virtual assistants like Siri, Alexa, and Google Assistant employ speech reputation to device voice instructions and provide responses.

Speech popularity is employed in numerous industries, which includes clinical and jail, to transcribe audio recordings into written text.

Speech recognition technology is covered into productivity software program, allowing customers to dictate text and manage packages the usage of voice commands.

Speech reputation enhances accessibility for people with disabilities, permitting them to interact with generation via speech.

NLP and Speech Recognition have superior notably with the advent of deep gaining knowledge of and neural community-based definitely fashions. As those technologies keep to evolve, they maintain the promise of facilitating seamless human-gadget communique, remodeling industries, and enhancing client reports across diverse packages.

2.3.3 Artificial Intelligence-Assisted Healthcare Services

Artificial Intelligence (AI) has emerged as a transformative stress inside the area of healthcare, revolutionizing how clinical services are added and improving affected character results. AI-assisted healthcare services leverage the strength of advanced algorithms, device reading, and records analytics to beautify clinical preference-making, diagnosis, remedy, and patient care.

AI-powered scientific imaging performs a essential function in early illness detection and analysis. Machine mastering algorithms examine scientific photographs, which include X-rays, MRIs, and CT scans, with extremely good accuracy. AI systems can discover abnormalities, tumors, and different anomalies, supporting physicians make extra informed selections and enhancing the accuracy of diagnosis.

AI helps personalized remedy plans for patients based totally on their medical records, genetic makeup, and response to treatments. By reading top notch quantities of affected person records, AI structures can expect treatment consequences and recommend the handiest restoration techniques tailored to each man or woman's desires. This technique ensures greater targeted and green treatments, main to higher affected person consequences.

AI is accelerating the drug discovery system through reading sizeable molecular datasets and predicting capability drug candidates. AI algorithms identify molecules with particular houses that can be powerful in treating severa diseases. This way expedites drug development, lowering costs and growing the hazard of finding new and progressive remedies.

AI-driven digital fitness assistants and chatbots offer sufferers with personalised healthcare steering and help. These virtual assistants can answer scientific questions, offer medicinal drug reminders, and provide way of lifestyles guidelines. They improve patient engagement and permit get right of entry to to healthcare facts each time and everywhere.

AI-based predictive analytics observe affected person statistics to discover people at excessive danger of growing positive clinical situations. This early identity enables proactive interventions, allowing healthcare providers to save you the development of sicknesses and reduce hospitalizations.

AI-powered some distance off affected person monitoring solutions allow non-prevent tracking of patients' health reputation out of doors traditional healthcare settings.

Wearable devices and sensors collect affected man or woman information, that is analyzed in real-time. Healthcare experts can then intrude directly if any abnormalities are detected, improving affected individual safety and allowing more green care shipping.

AI optimizes healthcare operations by way of streamlining administrative duties, handling patient appointments, and automating recurring techniques. This improved efficiency allows healthcare professionals to recognition extra on patient care and decreases administrative burdens.

While AI has amazing capability in healthcare, it additionally raises ethical concerns and information privacy troubles. Safeguarding affected character data and ensuring that AI structures adhere to ethical recommendations are essential to maintaining don't forget and ensuring the responsible use of AI in healthcare.

AI-assisted healthcare services are transforming the medical panorama by means of manner of improving analysis accuracy, personalizing remedies, rushing up drug improvement, and enhancing patient care. As AI keeps to increase, it'll play an more and more essential function in shaping the destiny of healthcare, making it extra green, to be had, and affected person-centric. However, responsible implementation, statistics privateness, and moral concerns stay paramount to make sure that AI technology definitely effect the healthcare enterprise and make a contribution to better fitness effects for people and groups worldwide.

CHAPTER 3

Human-Machine Collaboration

3.1 The Role of Artificial Intelligence in Collaboration with Humans

3.1.1 Combining Human and Artificial Intelligence Abilities

The integration of human intelligence and synthetic intelligence (AI) is a all of sudden evolving frontier that holds incredible promise in numerous fields and industries. Combining the precise strengths of each humans and machines can bring about powerful synergies, amplifying abilities and addressing complex demanding conditions.

The cause of blending human and AI abilties isn't always to replace human intelligence however to boost it. AI can procedure and analyze full-size portions of information at awesome speeds, presenting valuable insights and supporting human beings in choice-making strategies. Humans, however, own creativity, emotional intelligence, and intuition, which might be hard for machines to replicate. The synergy amongst human and AI abilities lets in for a more holistic approach to hassle-solving and desire-making.

AI excels in facts processing, sample reputation, and statistics-pushed predictions. By leveraging AI algorithms, humans can approach and examine complex statistics units with more performance and accuracy. This is mainly useful in fields like healthcare, finance, and medical research, in which massive volumes of records need to be analyzed to derive full-size insights.

When combining human and AI abilties, it's miles vital to adopt a human-targeted design method. AI structures must be purchaser-friendly, obvious, and interpretable to foster trust and attractiveness amongst human customers. Additionally, knowledge human choices, wishes, and limitations is crucial in designing AI structures that effectively complement human intelligence.

While AI can excel in narrow and well-described obligations, human creativity remains unparalleled. By taking part with AI tools, human beings can harness the energy of information-driven insights to inspire creative problem-fixing. AI-generated tips and mind can serve as a springboard for human creativity, essential to trendy answers and breakthroughs.

Integrating human and AI abilties moreover brings moral troubles to the leading aspect. Ensuring that AI systems align with human values, uphold privacy rights, and avoid bias is crucial. Ethical recommendations and regulations should be in location to control the responsible use of AI in combination with human intelligence.

The destiny of blending human and AI abilities lies in putting in seamless human-device collaboration. This involves developing intuitive interfaces, natural language processing, and adaptive AI structures that could understand and respond to human intentions efficaciously. Human-tool collaboration might be critical in fields like robotics, self sustaining structures, and virtual reality applications.

By leveraging AI gear, human beings can beautify their competencies and collect new records greater effectively. AI-powered learning structures can customise academic content, adapt to person gaining knowledge of styles, and provide personalized comments, revolutionizing education and lifetime learning.

The integration of human and AI capabilities will genuinely reshape the personnel landscape. As AI takes on repetitive and mundane obligations, human humans can consciousness on higher-order duties that require creativity, emotional intelligence, and important thinking. This shift will necessitate non-forestall gaining knowledge of and reskilling to conform to the evolving wishes of the technique market.

Combining human and synthetic intelligence talents opens up thrilling opportunities for innovation and progress. Embracing a collaborative approach, in which humans and machines supplement every special's strengths, can lead to transformative advancements in severa domains. However, ensuring responsible AI integration, upholding moral requirements, and prioritizing human-targeted design are vital for harnessing the total capability of this synergistic dating amongst human and AI intelligence. As we move ahead, embracing the capability of human-AI collaboration can launch a ultra-modern generation of possibilities and power exceptional alternate in society.

3.1.2 The Importance of Collaboration-Oriented Work Environments

Collaboration is a vital element in cutting-edge places of work that drives productiveness, innovation, and familiar success. Creating a piece environment that fosters collaboration amongst employees has become a strategic vital for organizations. Here, we discover the importance of selling collaboration within the place of job and the fine impact it can have on people and corporations.

When employees collaborate, they carry approximately together their severa talents, knowledge, and perspectives to tackle complicated demanding situations. This collective attempt leads to greater entire hassle-fixing and well-knowledgeable desire-making.

Collaboration nurtures a lifestyle of innovation and creativity. When humans artwork collectively, they encourage every different, sparking new mind and procedures to problems. This culture of creativity fosters non-stop improvement and continues groups at the leading edge in their industries.

Collaboration strengthens employee engagement via fostering a enjoy of belonging and fee. When employees collaborate, they revel in desired for their contributions, foremost to elevated method satisfaction and determination to the enterprise company's goals.

A collaborative art work environment encourages non-stop studying and expert development. Employees have the opportunity to observe from their colleagues, percentage information, and collect new abilities, contributing to their person growth and the business corporation's understanding.

Effective collaboration enhances conversation and interpersonal abilties amongst employees. As they art work collectively, they broaden higher teamwork and cooperation, which interprets into improved interactions and reduced conflicts.

Collaboration lets in businesses to adapt and thrive in a abruptly converting company landscape. It fosters flexibility and resilience, permitting corporations to reply quick to annoying situations and seize emerging opportunities.

Building believe and camaraderie is a herbal final results of collaboration. Trust is the muse of a achievement teamwork, permitting employees to depend upon every other's know-how and assist. A collaborative surroundings moreover creates a high quality place of job surroundings, forging robust relationships amongst group individuals.

Collaboration aligns individuals closer to shared targets. It guarantees that every one employees recognize the business enterprise's desires and the way their contributions make a contribution to its success. This shared imaginative and prescient instills a feel of reason and collective ownership in accomplishing organizational milestones.

A collaboration-oriented paintings environment is quintessential to an organisation's achievement. Collaboration complements hassle-fixing, fosters innovation, and drives worker engagement. Creating a way of life of collaboration outcomes in a extremely good and pleasing place of business wherein people can thrive, contributing their exceptional art work to obtain shared dreams.

3.2 The Use of Artificial Intelligence and Its Effects within the Workplace

3.2.1 The Impact of Artificial Intelligence on Productivity and Workflow

Artificial Intelligence (AI) has emerged as a transformative strain in the realm of productiveness and workflow optimization. As businesses attempting to find strategies to live aggressive and decorate overall performance, AI generation have installed to be valuable tools.

One of the most full-size contributions of AI to productiveness is automation. AI algorithms can manage repetitive and time-eating obligations, liberating up valuable human resources to consciousness on greater complex and strategic sports. Whether it's information get right of entry to, customer service inquiries, or ordinary evaluation, AI automation speeds up strategies, reducing manual effort and human mistakes.

AI-pushed records analysis allows groups to extract treasured insights from vast datasets. Advanced machine studying algorithms can understand styles, trends, and correlations inside facts that people might also pass over. These insights offer precious facts for choice-making and method development, empowering groups to make statistics-driven selections.

By integrating AI era into workflows, groups can streamline techniques and reap more performance. AI can pick out bottlenecks, optimize assignment allocation, or even are awaiting destiny beneficial resource necessities, ensuring that workflows are properly-organized and seamless.

AI's potential to system and examine huge quantities of information allows greater personalization for customers and customers. Through personalized tips and tailor-made evaluations, groups can enhance patron satisfaction and loyalty, ultimately leading to multiplied productivity and income.

AI-powered gadget can manner statistics in real-time, allowing fast selection-making. With get admission to to up to date statistics and predictive analytics, groups can respond unexpectedly to changing market conditions and make agile choices, gaining a aggressive aspect.

AI-powered herbal language processing (NLP) gear facilitate communication and collaboration inside organizations. NLP-enabled chatbots and virtual assistants streamline internal communique, supplying short get proper of entry to to records and solutions to queries, similarly improving productivity.

AI's predictive talents amplify beyond information evaluation. In enterprise settings, AI can anticipate tool screw ups and renovation goals, permitting corporations to perform preventive upkeep, lower downtime, and optimize resource allocation.

AI-powered customer support solutions enhance responsiveness and efficiency. Chatbots and virtual assistants can cope with consumer inquiries promptly, providing 24/7 support. This no longer pleasant improves client delight but moreover allows human retailers to recognition on greater complicated issues, developing standard productivity.

AI structures can studies from ancient records and purchaser interactions, constantly enhancing their usual overall performance. This adaptability ensures that AI technology become an increasing number of powerful over time, principal to ongoing enhancements in productiveness and workflow optimization.

AI's effect on productivity and workflow optimization is first rate and multi-faceted. Through automation, records evaluation, and higher personalization, AI empowers agencies to streamline operations and make facts-driven picks. The integration of AI technologies into workflows lets in real-time choice-making and efficient customer service, at the same time as additionally assisting continuous gaining knowledge of and improvement. Embracing AI as a productiveness-improving tool is crucial for organizations looking for to stay competitive and power innovation in brand new rapid-paced commercial enterprise landscape.

3.2.2 Implications at the Workforce and Employment

The huge adoption of artificial intelligence (AI) era has tremendous implications for the staff and employment landscape. While AI affords opportunities for improved productiveness and performance, it also increases issues about process displacement and the converting nature of exertions.

The upward push of AI-powered automation may also result in the displacement of certain jobs which may be vulnerable to automation. Roles that contain repetitive obligations and routine statistics processing are at higher danger of being changed by means of AI structures. However, it's far critical to apprehend that AI also can bring about the transformation of pastime roles, in which humans collaborate with AI era to enhance productiveness and desire-making.

As AI era continues to conform, the demand for emblem spanking new abilities within the staff emerges. Upskilling and reskilling grow to be critical for personnel to adapt to converting task necessities and stay applicable within the assignment market. Workers will want to acquire abilties related to AI development, information evaluation, and human-system collaboration to take advantage of recent opportunities.

Rather than changing humans totally, AI is much more likely to enhance human abilties and create a collaborative human-AI group of workers. AI technology can deal with repetitive responsibilities and records assessment, while human employees interest on duties that require creativity, emotional intelligence, and complex trouble-solving. Human-AI collaboration ends in extra green and powerful artwork methods.

The good sized adoption of AI raises ethical and societal worries. Ensuring that AI structures characteristic ethically, transparently, and without reinforcing biases is crucial. Additionally, policymakers ought to cope with issues related to statistics privateness, challenge displacement, and the impact of AI on society. Responsible AI development and implementation are vital for shaping a amazing destiny group of workers.

While AI can also additionally update certain jobs, it also creates new assignment possibilities in industries associated with AI development, implementation, and protection. Emerging sectors that depend on AI, along with self sufficient vehicles and AI-driven healthcare, provide thrilling career opportunities for employees with relevant competencies.

AI cannot reflect human trends like empathy, creativity, and interpersonal abilties. As AI handles greater routine tasks, the decision for for employees with excessive-degree cognitive and emotional capabilities will boom. Strong interpersonal competencies, adaptability, and hassle-fixing aptitude turn out to be treasured property inside the AI-augmented team of workers.

The impact of AI at the workforce varies at some point of agency sectors. Some industries benefit from AI's statistics evaluation and automation talents, foremost to progressed efficiency. In contrast, industries intently reliant on guide exertions can also experience large method displacement demanding situations.

Governments and policymakers play a essential position in preparing the team of workers for the AI-driven economic system. Implementing regulations that help upskilling and reskilling projects, promoting ethical AI use, and supplying help for displaced humans are important steps in addressing the workforce implications of AI.

AI's impact at the group of workers and employment is complicated and multifaceted. While venture displacement is a scenario, AI additionally creates new opportunities and desires for specialised abilities. Embracing a collaborative human-AI body of workers, prioritizing upskilling, and addressing moral considerations are important for maximizing the blessings of

AI at the same time as mitigating capability demanding situations within the destiny of hard work.

3.3 Areas Where Artificial Intelligence Can Assist in Daily Life

3.3.1 Personal Assistants and Smart Devices

Personal assistants and clever gadgets have grow to be an important part of current lifestyles, revolutionizing the manner we interact with generation and carry out daily duties. These AI-powered era offer comfort, overall performance, and custom designed reviews, making them more and more well-known amongst customers.

Personal assistants, which includes Siri, Google Assistant, and Amazon's Alexa, are designed to make our lives extra available and green. Through voice commands, users can perform various tasks, which incorporates setting reminders, sending messages, making calls, and controlling smart home devices, with minimum attempt.

One of the critical thing benefits of private assistants is their palms-unfastened operation. Users can engage with those AI-powered assistants via voice commands, putting off the need to bodily have interaction with devices. This function is particularly beneficial in situations wherein clients' hands are occupied or once they have mobility demanding situations.

Personal assistants play a vital characteristic in the growth of clever houses. By connecting with diverse smart gadgets, which encompass clever lighting, thermostats, and protection cameras, private assistants enable users to manipulate their domestic environment seamlessly. This integration complements home automation and strength overall performance.

AI-powered personal assistants leverage gadget gaining knowledge of algorithms to apprehend clients' preferences and conduct. Over time, they provide customized responses and tips, tailoring their interactions to every body's specific desires and possibilities.

Personal assistants feature a enormous reservoir of records, supplying on the spot answers to clients' questions. By having access to on-line databases and serps, they may deliver actual-time statistics on numerous subjects, from climate forecasts to ancient facts.

Smart gadgets, which include smartwatches and smartphones, are ready with personal assistant functionalities that improve productivity. Users can schedule appointments, set alarms, manipulate calendars, and get entry to important facts at the go.

Personal assistants allow voice change, allowing customers to keep and make purchases using voice instructions. This characteristic is an increasing number of well-known among clients, offering a continuing and efficient buying enjoy.

Smart gadgets and private assistants contribute to more accessibility and inclusivity for customers with disabilities. Voice-based totally interactions provide an opportunity method of communique and interaction, making generation more reachable to a miles wider variety of clients.

Personal assistants can offer amusement by means of the usage of gambling track, studying audiobooks, and presenting guidelines for films and TV indicates. Users also can use voice commands to manipulate their media gadgets and get entry to their preferred content material.

AI-powered personal assistants constantly improve via consumer interactions and feedback. As they accumulate greater statistics and insights, they come to be better at records clients' dreams and delivering more correct and beneficial responses.

Personal assistants and clever gadgets have converted the way we interact with technology and perform every day responsibilities. Their convenience, efficiency, and personalised reports have made them an crucial a part of our lives. As AI generation continues to boost, we can expect even extra state-of-the-art and bendy personal assistants and smart gadgets that cater to our ever-evolving desires and choices.

3.3.2 Entertainment and Interaction with Artificial Intelligence

Artificial Intelligence (AI) has revolutionized the entertainment company, offering new and immersive studies for clients. From interactive storytelling to AI-powered virtual characters, the combination of AI in amusement has reshaped how we engage with content.

AI algorithms look at patron alternatives, viewing behavior, and interactions to supply custom designed content suggestions. Streaming platforms like Netflix and YouTube leverage AI to signify movies, TV shows, and motion pictures tailored to person tastes, ensuring an attractive and fun entertainment revel in.

AI plays a first-rate characteristic in interactive storytelling and gaming. AI-pushed narratives adapt based on person options and actions, presenting custom designed storylines and gameplay reports. This degree of interactivity will growth consumer engagement and adds replay charge to video video games and interactive storytelling testimonies.

AI technology are able to generating content material autonomously. For example, AI can compose song, create artwork, or even write tales and scripts. This opens up new opportunities for content cloth advent and creative expression, blurring the lines amongst human creativity and AI-generated works.

Entertainment now features AI-powered digital characters that may have interaction with clients in various methods. Virtual assistants like chatbots and digital influencers can interact in conversations, solution questions, and entertain customers thru social media systems and programs.

AI can look at human emotions and sentiments from various sources, inclusive of social media posts and person interactions. This sentiment evaluation lets in content material material creators and entrepreneurs apprehend target audience reactions to their artwork, letting them tailor content to resonate higher with viewers.

Voice assistants, along with Amazon's Alexa and Apple's Siri, have end up vital factors of smart gadgets. Users may have interaction with those AI-driven assistants to get proper of entry to records, control smart domestic devices, and carry out diverse duties, presenting a continuing and interactive enjoy.

AI enhances virtual and augmented fact opinions via developing realistic and responsive virtual environments. AI algorithms enable digital characters to recognize and reply to user gestures, developing more immersive and interactive digital reality reports.

AI assists content material material creators in video improving, special effects, and put up-manufacturing duties. AI-powered equipment can automate repetitive obligations, decorate visible results, and optimize content material for distinctive systems, streamlining the content fabric advent way.

AI technology have even entered the area of live performances. Musicians and artists use AI to create interactive performances, wherein AI responds to target audience inputs and influences the show in actual-time.

AI-powered virtual social structures permit customers to engage and socialize in digital environments. These systems create possibilities for virtual social gatherings, activities, and collaboration, expanding the concept of social interactions past physical limitations.

AI's integration in amusement has transformed how we consume and engage with content material cloth. From personalised hints to AI-generated content material and digital characters, AI enhances amusement reports, offering customers new stages of interactivity and engagement. As AI era continues to comply, we are capable of count on even more current and immersive entertainment evaluations that redefine the boundaries of human-AI interplay in the international of amusement.

CHAPTER 4

The Societal Impact of Artificial Intelligence

4.1 The Impact of Artificial Intelligence on the Labor Market and Unemployment

4.1.1 Effects of Artificial Intelligence on Occupations and Industries

The massive adoption of artificial intelligence (AI) is reshaping occupations and industries in the course of the globe. AI's transformative skills provide severa blessings, along with expanded performance and productivity, but also boost problems approximately pastime displacement and group of workers version.

AI technology excel at automating repetitive and everyday tasks that don't require complicated desire-making. This automation influences numerous industries, from manufacturing and logistics to customer support and facts entry, leading to increased performance and decreased labor prices.

AI's statistics analysis competencies have a profound impact on industries including finance, advertising and marketing, and healthcare. By processing giant amounts of records and identifying styles and tendencies, AI allows specialists make statistics-pushed alternatives, improving outcomes and aid allocation.

The creation of AI-pushed automation might also result in technique displacement for certain occupations. Workers in roles which may be specially repetitive and with out issues automatic face the threat of activity loss. However, this shift additionally creates possibilities for reskilling and upskilling, permitting workers to transition to new roles that complement AI technology.

While AI can also replace a few procedure roles, it moreover creates new possibilities. AI development, protection, and implementation require specialized abilities, main to method advent in areas related to AI technologies. Emerging fields, inclusive of AI ethics, AI consulting, and AI-assisted creativity, offer capability for brand new career paths.

Rather than fully changing human humans, AI often collaborates with humans to enhance productivity and choice-making. This collaborative technique allows human people to attention on responsibilities that require creativity, emotional intelligence, and complex trouble-fixing, at the equal time as AI handles everyday duties.

AI's impact on healthcare is some distance-carrying out, from AI-pushed analysis and remedy pointers to streamlining administrative obligations. AI-powered medical imaging and diagnostic device offer faster and additional correct checks, enhancing affected man or woman results.

AI is reworking schooling and schooling practices. AI-powered adaptive getting to know structures provide personalised mastering critiques, catering to individual pupil wishes and abilties. Additionally, AI is increasingly more utilized in company schooling and expert improvement packages.

AI is making its mark in innovative industries, together with tune, art, and content material advent. AI-generated artwork, track compositions, and content material cloth recommendation algorithms are tough traditional notions of creativity and pushing the bounds of human-AI collaboration.

AI is revolutionizing transportation and logistics industries through the improvement of self sustaining motors and optimized logistics structures. Self-the usage of automobiles and AI-powered drones promise greater inexperienced transportation and delivery services.

The integration of AI into various occupations and industries increases ethical and regulatory issues. Concerns regarding information privateness, bias in AI algorithms, and the responsible use of AI must be addressed to ensure honest and ethical AI implementation.

The consequences of synthetic intelligence on occupations and industries are multifaceted. While AI-pushed automation might also moreover cause activity displacement in a few regions, it additionally creates new opportunities and needs for specialised competencies. Human-AI collaboration and the transformation of industries present interesting opportunities for improved performance and innovation. As AI era maintains to comply, policymakers, corporations, and workers must collaborate to navigate the converting panorama of labor and ensure a future in which AI blessings society and the personnel as a whole.

4.1.2 New Job Opportunities and Skill Transformation

The rapid development of synthetic intelligence (AI) is ushering in a brand new technology of method opportunities and talent transformation. As AI technologies emerge as greater trendy during industries, they devise name for for specialized roles and necessitate the development of latest skill sets.

With the developing use of AI in diverse applications, the demand for AI developers and programmers is on the upward thrust. These professionals are responsible for designing, building, and imposing AI algorithms and structures. Expertise in tool learning, statistics technological know-how, and programming languages like Python and R are essential in this discipline.

Data analysts and scientists play a essential feature within the AI-driven economic device. They are chargeable for gathering, processing, and studying big datasets to derive insights and help statistics-pushed choice-making. Proficiency in records manipulation, statistical evaluation, and records visualization are important skills in this area.

The ethical issues surrounding AI utilization necessitate the emergence of AI ethicists and coverage experts. These specialists are accountable for ensuring that AI systems perform ethically, transparently, and without reinforcing biases. They play a key feature in growing tips and tips for responsible AI deployment.

As AI more and more collaborates with human personnel, there's a want for experts who can facilitate powerful human-AI interactions. These specialists bridge the gap between AI technology and human customers, ensuring seamless integration and maximizing the benefits of AI-human collaboration.

As businesses are trying to find to leverage AI for competitive gain, AI specialists and strategists are in excessive name for. These experts suggest agencies on AI implementation strategies, take a look at potential use times, and manual the integration of AI era into present approaches.

With the accelerated use of AI, the want for cybersecurity professionals is greater said. These specialists protect AI systems from cyber threats, making sure data privacy and safeguarding AI-powered packages from malicious assaults.

In the AI-pushed economic system, supplying amazing consumer opinions is paramount. Customer experience analysts leverage AI-pushed insights to understand purchaser possibilities and behavior, allowing companies to offer customized and tailor-made services.

AI-powered robotics and automation are reworking industries like manufacturing, logistics, and healthcare. Robotics and automation engineers format, extend, and hold AI-driven robot structures to optimize processes and increase performance.

AI is likewise influencing the innovative industries. Content curators and creatives collaborate with AI technologies to develop compelling content material and customized studies for clients. AI-generated art, tune, and content material hints mission traditional notions of creativity.

As AI becomes more incorporated into numerous factors of life, there is a developing want for professionals who can navigate emotional intelligence in human-AI interactions. Emotional intelligence professionals help design AI systems which can empathize and reply correctly to human feelings.

The upward push of AI necessitates a shift within the competencies demanded within the employees. As regular duties are automated, there's an accelerated recognition on capabilities that supplement AI technologies. Skills like emotional intelligence, vital questioning, creativity, trouble-solving, adaptability, and complex conversation end up greater valuable, as they will be hard for AI to replicate.

The AI-pushed monetary system is developing new activity opportunities and reworking ability necessities during industries. AI developers, records analysts, ethicists, and human-AI collaboration specialists are among the new roles emerging in reaction to AI's integration. Additionally, abilities like emotional intelligence, creativity, and complex hassle-solving benefit significance as they decorate human-AI collaboration and complement AI generation. Embracing capability transformation and fostering knowledge in AI-associated fields are essential for humans and organizations on the lookout for to thrive inside the evolving process market fashioned with the useful resource of AI technologies.

4.2 The Role of Artificial Intelligence in Economy and Trade

4.2.1 Artificial Intelligence's Effects on Production and Efficiency

Artificial Intelligence (AI) is revolutionizing production techniques and riding substantial improvements in efficiency for the duration of various industries. From streamlining manufacturing operations to optimizing supply chain manipulate, AI's transformative skills have a profound impact on productivity and operational normal performance.

AI allows superior automation in production approaches. Robots and AI-powered machines can carry out complicated obligations with precision and tempo, reducing the need for human intervention in repetitive and risky sports. This automation leads to extended manufacturing fees, reduced mistakes, and greater perfect place of business safety.

AI-pushed predictive protection structures display screen device and equipment in real-time, studying data to are watching for functionality failures before they arise. By figuring out maintenance desires proactively, organizations can decrease downtime, optimize protection schedules, and extend the lifespan in their belongings.

AI optimizes deliver chain control via reading massive quantities of facts to make accurate call for forecasts, optimize inventory ranges, and find out the most inexperienced transportation routes. These insights assist agencies reduce lead times, manipulate stock prices, and enhance typical deliver chain performance.

AI-powered notable manipulate structures can check out products and materials with excessive precision, detecting defects and deviations from exquisite requirements. Early disease detection reduces waste and ensures that simplest remarkable merchandise attain the marketplace, enhancing patron pride and brand recognition.

AI algorithms look at manufacturing records and market traits to optimize aid allocation and production making plans. Businesses can regulate manufacturing schedules, inventory degrees, and body of workers allocation in real-time, responding to changing wishes and market conditions correctly.

AI conducts in-depth evaluation of producing strategies, identifying areas for development and optimization. By optimizing workflows and getting rid of inefficiencies, companies can acquire higher productiveness and reduce production expenses.

AI contributes to power efficiency in production with the useful resource of optimizing power consumption and beneficial aid utilization. Smart strength management systems powered via AI algorithms make sure that electricity is used successfully, lowering operational fees and environmental effect.

AI-driven manufacturing structures permit mass customization and personalization of merchandise. By studying purchaser alternatives and statistics, agencies can tailor merchandise to character dreams, improving consumer pleasure and loyalty.

AI expedites the product improvement and innovation approach. By studying marketplace inclinations and client remarks, organizations can hastily growth and release new merchandise, gaining a aggressive aspect with quicker time-to-marketplace.

AI's potential to research and adapt through the years fosters continuous improvement in manufacturing processes. AI structures analyze statistics and overall performance metrics, identifying possibilities for refinement and optimization, main to ongoing improvements in production performance.

AI's consequences on manufacturing and overall performance are a long way-reaching and transformative. From advanced automation and predictive protection to supply chain optimization and energy efficiency, AI technology offer notable blessings at some stage in industries. By leveraging AI to streamline production strategies and optimize useful resource allocation, corporations can reap better productivity, lessen costs, and live aggressive inside the dynamic and speedy-paced global market. Embracing AI-powered answers is important for agencies searching for to thrive within the digital age and harness the complete functionality of AI to drive manufacturing and operational excellence.

4.2.2 Use of Artificial Intelligence in Trade and Marketing

Artificial Intelligence (AI) is reshaping the panorama of trade and marketing and marketing, revolutionizing the way organizations have interaction with clients, make information-driven picks, and optimize advertising and marketing strategies. By leveraging AI-powered technologies, corporations can benefit precious insights, deliver customized reports, and enhance their aggressive region.

AI permits businesses to investigate massive quantities of purchaser data, which include purchase statistics, alternatives, and on-line interactions. By leveraging device studying algorithms, businesses can benefit treasured insights into client behavior, figuring out patterns and developments that tell centered advertising and marketing strategies.

AI-powered advice engines supply customized content material and product guidelines to person customers based on their alternatives and former interactions. This diploma of personalization enhances client engagement and increases the threat of conversion and repeat commercial enterprise.

AI-powered chatbots and virtual assistants offer real-time customer support and assist. By answering patron inquiries and resolving issues proper away, organizations can beautify consumer delight and decorate the overall purchaser enjoy.

AI generation help in sales and lead technology thru figuring out capacity clients who are much more likely to transform. Through predictive analytics, businesses can prioritize leads, optimize sales funnels, and tailor their advertising and marketing efforts to aim high-value opportunities.

AI-powered pricing algorithms have a look at market conditions, competitor pricing, and purchaser call for to optimize product pricing. Dynamic pricing techniques primarily based on actual-time records help organizations remain aggressive and maximize sales.

AI equipment show social media systems to song brand mentions and client sentiment. Sentiment assessment lets in agencies to gauge public notion, identify purchaser ache elements, and respond directly to remarks and concerns.

AI generation are able to generating content material, which includes articles, product descriptions, and social media posts. Content curation algorithms can also curate relevant content material fabric from numerous resources to have interaction audiences and foster concept control.

AI permits companies improve their seo strategies by way of analyzing are trying to find engine algorithms and patron behavior. AI-driven seo gear provide treasured insights to optimize internet site content and improve searching for engine scores.

AI-powered e mail marketing systems use machine mastering to investigate purchaser conduct and optimize e-mail campaigns. These structures can suggest the best time to ship emails, personalize content cloth, and enhance e mail open and click-thru charges.

AI streamlines marketplace studies with the useful resource of collecting and reading statistics from diverse sources. AI-pushed aggressive evaluation equipment offer groups with treasured intelligence on opposition' strategies and marketplace developments.

The use of AI in change and advertising and advertising offers super benefits for corporations searching out to thrive in the virtual age. By leveraging AI technology for purchaser insights, customized marketing, chatbot help, and pricing optimization, businesses can enhance customer testimonies, growth earnings, and benefit a competitive facet. AI's programs in content material advent, search engine advertising and marketing, e-mail advertising, and market research moreover offer precious equipment for groups to live in advance of market traits and adapt to changing customer behaviors. Embracing AI-powered answers in exchange and advertising is crucial for businesses looking for to remain applicable and a hit in an an increasing number of data-pushed and competitive marketplace.

4.3 Potential Changes in Social Dynamics Due to Artificial Intelligence

4.3.1 Social Perception and Interaction with Artificial Intelligence

As synthetic intelligence (AI) will become extra integrated into our daily lives, our perceptions of and interactions with AI are evolving. AI-powered technology, which consist of virtual assistants and chatbots, are becoming increasingly more frequent, shaping how we have interaction with machines and the way we apprehend them.

One of the captivating additives of human-AI interplay is the tendency to anthropomorphize AI structures. When AI virtual assistants or chatbots have human-like functions of their interactions, human beings may additionally extend emotional attachments to them. This emotional connection can lead users to view AI as greater than most effective a device, attributing human-like traits and personalities to the machines.

The social perception of AI is induced with the aid of the quantity of believe and reliability customers place in the ones systems. As AI technology come to be greater modern day and exhibit accurate responses, users have a propensity to rely on them for various duties, predominant to elevated trust in their abilties.

As AI will become greater worried in desire-making strategies, ethical and moral issues come into play. Users and society at large grapple with questions of AI ethics, consisting of duty for AI's moves, bias in AI algorithms, and the moral implications of AI-powered selections.

The developing integration of AI in severa industries increases troubles about method displacement and the capability effect on the frame of employees. Some people perceive AI as a danger to task safety, fearing that AI might also moreover update human workers in sure roles.

Positive person studies with AI technology enhance social belief and reputation. AI systems that provide custom designed interactions and tailor responses to individual picks are more likely to be nicely-obtained through users.

The notion of human-AI collaboration is gaining significance as AI is increasingly more included into various elements of labor and daily life. Instead of seeing AI as a alternative for human abilities, the point of interest is shifting in the direction of how people and AI can collaborate to gain better outcomes.

The societal effect of AI is a subject of ongoing discussions. As AI technology impact numerous additives of society, which include privateness, protection, and healthcare, humans's perceptions of AI are motivated through the perceived advantages and dangers it brings.

AI structures can inadvertently perpetuate biases gift in the facts used to educate them. The attention of AI bias has prompted increased scrutiny of AI technology and a name for equity and transparency in their improvement and deployment.

AI era that simulate emotional guide or companionship, including digital pets or chatbots, can have an impact on humans's social belief of AI. These structures may additionally provide comfort and companionship, especially for folks that may additionally additionally experience lonely or remoted.

Promoting education and interest approximately AI's competencies and boundaries is important for shaping social perception. As individuals end up greater knowledgeable about AI technology, they're higher organized to engage with AI systems appreciably and responsibly.

The social belief and interplay with synthetic intelligence are multifaceted and constantly evolving. As AI technology become greater integrated into our lives, the way we apprehend and engage with AI will keep to form our courting with the ones shrewd systems. Promoting moral concerns, fostering superb person reviews, and galvanizing human-AI collaboration are crucial in constructing a harmonious and useful coexistence amongst people and AI era in society.

4.3.2 Cultural and Social Norms Influenced via manner of Artificial Intelligenc

Artificial Intelligence (AI) is not simplest remodeling industries and generation however additionally exerting a good sized impact on cultural and social norms. As AI era emerge as greater embedded in our every day lives, they shape how we interact, communicate, and recognize the arena spherical us.

AI-powered communique equipment, which includes chatbots and virtual assistants, are changing the way we have interaction with technology and every other. People are increasingly carrying out conversational interactions with AI, which has the functionality to redefine the norms of communication in numerous contexts.

AI's capacity to research huge portions of statistics has raised worries approximately privacy and records sharing. As AI systems collect and gadget personal statistics, cultural norms around records privacy and consent are being reevaluated and fashioned by means of the want for responsible statistics managing.

The automation of wonderful responsibilities with the resource of AI technology influences the conventional paintings-lifestyles balance. As repetitive and mundane responsibilities are handled by AI, there may be a ability shift in societal norms round paintings hours, enjoyment time, and the cost located on human difficult work.

AI's integration into various technologies is selling more accessibility and inclusivity. AI-powered equipment, along side speech popularity and text-to-speech applications, permit people with disabilities to get right of entry to statistics and participate more absolutely in society.

AI-driven content cloth curation and advice algorithms form what facts and content fabric customers are uncovered to on line. This has the potential to create echo chambers and have an effect on cultural norms by using the usage of reinforcing present ideals and alternatives.

As AI technologies produce innovative works, including artwork and song, cultural norms surrounding the idea of creativity and authorship are evolving. Debates stand up approximately the feature of AI in revolutionary expression and its impact on the art work and amusement industries.

AI structures can inadvertently perpetuate biases gift in the data they're professional on. This has sparked discussions approximately cultural biases in AI algorithms and the want for fairness and inclusivity in AI improvement.

As AI generation grow to be extra modern-day, society's degree of believe in these structures is evolving. Cultural norms around counting on AI for decision-making and accepting AI-generated hints are continuously converting.

The developing presence of AI in severa elements of existence increases questions about the character of human-AI relationships. As AI technology grow to be more interactive and human-like, cultural norms around social interactions with AI are being redefined.

AI's integration in schooling is converting how we method studying and expertise acquisition. AI-powered adaptive gaining knowledge of structures assignment conventional norms of observe room education with the resource of tailoring instructional research to character college students.

Artificial intelligence is reshaping cultural and social norms in numerous methods, from the way we talk and engage to how we fee privateness and creativity. As AI era preserve to growth, it's far important for society to engage in ongoing discussions about the moral, cultural, and social implications of AI's have an effect on. Establishing accountable hints and promoting cognizance throughout the cultural effect of AI will assist form a destiny in which the ones shrewd era without a doubt make a contribution to our cultural panorama and societal norms.

CHAPTER 5

Ethics and Artificial Intelligence

5.1 Ethical Issues and Responsibilities of Artificial Intelligence

5.1.1 Ethical Decision-Making Processes in Artificial Intelligence

Ethical choice-making is a essential factor of growing and deploying synthetic intelligence (AI) systems responsibly. As AI technology turn out to be increasingly integrated into numerous components of society, addressing moral issues is important to make sure that AI is advanced and utilized in a way that aligns with human values and societal well-being.

AI builders and researchers use ethical frameworks as guiding standards to shape the selection-making manner. These frameworks may additionally consist of standards collectively with equity, transparency, obligation, privacy, and the avoidance of harm. By adhering to such frameworks, AI practitioners motive to create systems that align with ethical requirements.

The ethical preference-making manner in AI includes considering diverse views and inputs. Engaging stakeholders from one in every of a type backgrounds, together with ethicists, policymakers, specialists, and affected groups, ensures that a big sort of viewpoints is taken under consideration.

Ethical AI improvement includes respecting data privacy and acquiring informed consent from humans whose statistics is used to teach AI models. Ensuring that records is amassed and used responsibly and transparently is crucial to hold accept as true with in AI systems.

AI algorithms can inadvertently perpetuate biases gift in the statistics used for schooling. Ethical selection-making includes ongoing efforts to understand and mitigate bias in AI structures, ensuring equity and equity in their results.

Ethical AI requires that the choice-making approach of AI structures be explainable and obvious. Users and stakeholders have to be capable of understand how AI arrived at a particular selection or advice, fostering believe and obligation.

Ethical AI selection-making emphasizes the importance of human oversight and manage over AI structures. Humans have to keep the functionality to interfere and override AI picks, particularly in critical contexts like healthcare and self sufficient vehicles.

AI ethics is an ongoing manner that calls for continuous tracking and evaluation of AI systems. Regular checks ensure that AI technology live aligned with ethical requirements as societal norms and values evolve.

Before deploying AI structures, conducting moral effect checks is essential. These assessments study capacity moral implications, risks, and societal outcomes of AI packages, allowing knowledgeable decision-making.

AI developers and implementers need to keep in mind cultural variations and contexts in their moral desire-making.

What can be taken into consideration moral in a single cultural putting won't be applicable in any other, and respecting cultural range is vital.

Collaboration amongst AI developers, policymakers, and the wider network is vital to cope with ethical demanding situations collectively. Establishing duty mechanisms ensures that moral requirements are upheld at some degree in the AI lifecycle.

Ethical decision-making techniques are essential to the accountable development and deployment of synthetic intelligence. By adhering to ethical frameworks, thinking about diverse perspectives, and addressing concerns which include statistics privacy, bias, and transparency, AI practitioners can create AI systems that align with ethical values and societal expectations. Continuously comparing and monitoring AI structures and attractive in ethical effect assessments are essential to ensure that AI technology make a contribution surely to society whilst mitigating ability risks and annoying situations. Embracing moral practices in AI development is important for shaping a destiny where AI technology decorate human well-being and contribute to a more inclusive and equitable society.

5.1.2 Bias and Discrimination Challenges

One of the maximum giant moral disturbing conditions in synthetic intelligence (AI) is the presence of bias and discrimination in AI systems. Despite AI's ability for independent choice-making, AI algorithms can inadvertently perpetuate or even make bigger societal biases gift inside the information used to teach them.

AI algorithms study from historic records, which might also reflect historical biases and inequalities. If the schooling facts is biased, the AI tool can mirror and strengthen those biases, essential to discriminatory effects.

Algorithmic bias refers to biases that emerge from the shape and layout of AI algorithms. Even if the schooling information is unbiased, the algorithms themselves can introduce bias due to the way they interpret and technique information.

AI structures can make alternatives that disproportionately impact positive agencies or people based totally totally on attributes collectively with race, gender, age, or socioeconomic fame. Discriminatory effects can cease end result from biased schooling facts or algorithmic choices.

The lack of range among AI developers and researchers can result in blind spots in identifying and addressing bias. Diverse views are essential in growing AI structures which might be truthful and equitable.

Black-field AI structures, where the selection-making method isn't obvious, should make it difficult to perceive and deal with bias. The lack of explainability hinders expertise how the AI arrived at sure selections.

Biased AI systems can create feedback loops, where discriminatory effects perpetuate further bias in the schooling records. This cycle can cause non-stop reinforcement of gift biases.

AI systems may additionally additionally conflict to recall the nuanced context of certain choices, predominant to biased judgments. The same desire made in extremely good contexts may additionally yield brilliant results, causing inconsistencies and capability unfairness.

Data shortage or negative facts high-quality in high-quality businesses can purpose underrepresentation and further increase bias. Inadequate example can result in skewed AI models.

AI systems may not properly account for intersectionality—the overlap of multiple social identities, which incorporates race, gender, and socioeconomic repute. Failure to recall intersectionality can motive compounded bias.

The unexpectedly evolving nature of AI technology poses worrying conditions for regulators and policymakers in addressing bias and discrimination. Creating powerful regulations to make certain ethical AI practices on the identical time as now not stifling innovation calls for cautious consideration.

Using diverse and consultant facts all through AI training can assist reduce bias and make certain extra equitable effects.

Developing algorithms and gear to discover and mitigate bias is vital. Techniques which incorporates antagonistic training and debiasing algorithms can assist reduce bias in AI models.

Promoting the improvement of explainable AI models can boom transparency and permit better understanding of AI picks.

Creating enterprise-extensive moral recommendations and necessities for AI development and deployment can foster responsible AI practices.

Ensuring that AI structures art work collaboratively with human oversight can assist cope with contextual biases and make complex selections greater equitable.

Regularly evaluating AI structures for bias and carrying out audits can assist discover and cope with bias over the years.

Encouraging variety in AI development organizations can carry precise perspectives to the table, predominant to greater robust and honest AI systems.

Engaging with affected corporations and stakeholders inside the development and deployment of AI structures can help understand functionality bias and make sure AI benefits all users.

Conducting moral effect assessments in advance than deploying AI systems can compare capability biases and discrimination dangers.

Implementing customer comments mechanisms can allow customers to record biased consequences and make a contribution to ongoing improvements in AI systems.

Addressing bias and discrimination stressful situations in AI is critical for building truthful and equitable AI structures. By selling diverse and representative records, adopting bias detection and mitigation techniques, and fostering transparency and human oversight, we can paintings closer to extra ethical and honest AI generation. The collaboration of stakeholders, such as AI developers, researchers, policymakers, and affected communities, is crucial in overcoming those demanding situations and creating a destiny wherein AI benefits all individuals and does now not perpetuate societal inequalities.

5.2 The Relationship Between Artificial Intelligence and Data Privacy

5.2.1 Data Collection and Personal Privacy

Data collection is the inspiration of artificial intelligence (AI) systems, permitting them to analyze, adapt, and make informed alternatives. However, the great accumulating and processing of personal records raise big problems approximately individual privateness and data protection.

AI structures rely upon massive quantities of information to function efficaciously. As more statistics is accrued from humans, concerns stand up approximately the quantity of records collection and capability privateness intrusions.

AI frequently deals with PII, collectively with names, addresses, economic facts, and health records. The coping with of such sensitive facts requires stringent privateness safeguards to save you unauthorized get right of entry to or misuse.

The aggregation of large datasets poses a danger of statistics breaches and cyberattacks, leading to the exposure of sensitive facts and capability privateness violations.

In some instances, human beings might not be sincerely privy to the data amassed approximately them or won't have given informed consent for its use in AI systems.

AI-powered algorithms can create focused profiles of human beings, main to invasive focused advertising and manipulation of customer conduct.

The use of AI in surveillance technology increases troubles approximately authorities tracking and ability infringement on civil liberties and human rights.

The centralization of statistics inside the arms of some powerful entities can cause facts monopolies and limit consumer control over their non-public records.

Even when facts is anonymized, re-identification techniques can also moreover hyperlink it decrease returned to particular people, posing dangers to privateness.

Global facts flows in AI raise demanding conditions in complying with one-of-a-kind privateness suggestions during international locations.

The moral use of data is essential in making sure that AI systems do not make the maximum or harm human beings via the misuse of personal records.

Adopting information minimization practices ensures that best crucial and relevant statistics is amassed, decreasing the danger of privateness violations.

Incorporating privateness concerns from the inception of AI systems allows construct privateness protections into the design and development method.

Obtaining knowledgeable consent from individuals for information collection and use ensures transparency and empowers clients to make knowledgeable selections about their data.

Implementing strong anonymization and encryption strategies can guard touchy records from unauthorized get right of access to.

Adhering to privateness regulations and enterprise requirements lets in ensure that AI systems have a look at criminal and ethical privacy requirements.

Giving customers extra control over their records and the ability to manage their privacy settings fosters a experience of empowerment and trust.

Conducting regular privateness audits can select out and deal with functionality privateness vulnerabilities in AI systems.

Raising public attention approximately records collection practices and privateness dangers empowers people to guard their privateness rights.

Promoting collaborative records governance frameworks concerning numerous stakeholders can make certain accountable and ethical facts use.

Conducting privacy effect assessments for AI projects can examine capability privateness dangers and manual the improvement of privacy-touchy solutions.

Data series is crucial to the functioning of AI structures, but it additionally raises significant challenges regarding private privateness. By enforcing records minimization practices, obtaining knowledgeable consent, and prioritizing privateness protections, we will cope with the ones demanding situations and make sure that AI respects man or woman privacy rights. Collaborative efforts among stakeholders, public attention, and adherence to privacy rules are essential in constructing AI systems that are not handiest sensible but moreover respectful of personal privacy and ethical facts use.

5.2.2 Ensuring Data Security and Protection with Artificial Intelligence

As artificial intelligence (AI) continues to transform industries and beautify diverse packages, ensuring information safety and safety becomes a paramount subject. AI systems depend heavily on information, frequently containing sensitive and precious records, making them attractive desires for cyberattacks and breaches.

AI systems are susceptible to cyber threats, such as records breaches, malware attacks, and denial-of-carrier (DoS) attacks. The growing complexity of AI algorithms and the interconnectedness of structures decorate the danger of protection vulnerabilities.

Implementing robust encryption techniques for statistics garage and transmission permits shield statistics from unauthorized get proper of access to and guarantees its confidentiality.

Employing MFA provides a in addition layer of safety with the resource of requiring customers to offer multiple varieties of authentication before gaining access to sensitive records or AI systems.

Using strong conversation protocols, which includes HTTPS, for records transmission prevents interception and eavesdropping of records at some point of transit.

Implementing granular get entry to controls ensures that fine legal personnel can get right of entry to precise records, lowering the risk of internal information breaches.

For AI structures deployed in the cloud, making sure the safety of cloud infrastructure is vital to defend facts from capacity cloud-based totally attacks.

Frequently updating AI software program and applying protection patches lets in cope with vulnerabilities and shield in opposition to recounted threats.

Leveraging AI for chance detection and anomaly detection can enhance the capacity to find out and respond to capability safety breaches.

Using privateness-keeping strategies like differential privateness or federated getting to know permits AI fashions to look at from data without straight away getting access to touchy statistics.

Implementing stable information disposal practices ensures that information is completely erased from garage devices while it isn't wished, decreasing the threat of information leaks.

Conducting regular protection audits and vulnerability tests enables emerge as aware of weaknesses in AI structures and data infrastructure.

Performing moral hacking through penetration checking out allows choose out potential entry factors for cyber attackers and check the resilience of AI structures.

Educating personnel approximately statistics safety tremendous practices and potential threats can prevent accidental records breaches due to human mistakes.

Collaborating with cybersecurity specialists and businesses enhances the potential to deal with sophisticated threats and put into effect nice practices.

Having a properly-described incident reaction plan in region allows fast and effective movement inside the occasion of a facts breach or cyber incident.

Implementing stable AI model deployment practices guarantees that AI structures do now not inadvertently divulge sensitive facts during operation.

Adhering to ethical concepts in information series and use enables make sure records is obtained and applied responsibly.

Complying with applicable statistics safety laws and policies reinforces the dedication to statistics security and privacy.

Regular data backups and disaster recovery plans mitigate the chance of records loss in the occasion of a breach or device failure.

Being transparent with customers approximately statistics handling practices builds accept as true with and self notion in the AI device's protection.

Safeguarding records safety and protection is a vital issue of deploying synthetic intelligence responsibly. By imposing sturdy encryption, get right of access to controls, and multi-issue authentication, groups can protect touchy statistics from cyber threats. Regular protection audits, employee schooling, and collaborative partnerships with cybersecurity professionals make more potent the overall safety posture of AI systems. Ethical use of records, compliance with guidelines, and obvious statistics handling practices enhance the commitment to records safety and privateness. As AI technology maintain to adapt, ongoing efforts to make sure records safety and safety will be critical in preserving the agree with of clients and fostering accountable AI deployment.

5.3 Implications of Artificial Intelligence on Justice and Equality

5.3.1 Artificial Intelligence's Contributions to Law and Justice Systems

Artificial Intelligence (AI) has made big contributions to severa industries, and the sphere of law and justice isn't any exception. AI's transformative capabilities are reshaping how prison professionals and justice systems function, streamlining techniques, improving choice-making, and improving access to justice.

AI-powered device can successfully examine big volumes of criminal files, which consist of case law, statutes, and policies. By rapidly identifying applicable precedents and jail arguments, AI streamlines felony research, saving time and assets for prison experts.

AI algorithms can analyze historical case statistics to count on the probable consequences of ongoing instances. Legal experts can use those insights to make informed choices and boom more potent litigation strategies.

AI-pushed settlement assessment equipment automate the assessment of contracts, figuring out essential terms and ability dangers. This complements the performance and accuracy of agreement management for agencies and prison groups.

AI-powered legal chatbots provide actual-time assist to people attempting to find prison information and steerage. These chatbots can solution commonplace criminal queries, offer crook recommendation, and direct users to suitable felony resources.

AI is being explored to help judges in making more regular and sincere sentencing selections. By studying relevant elements and historical information, AI can help determine the threat of recidivism and tell parole choices.

AI technology decorate the corporation and control of criminal instances with the useful resource of automating administrative responsibilities, scheduling, and monitoring time limits. This streamlines the workflow and improves average efficiency in prison processes.

AI-powered e-discovery platforms can sift via big volumes of digital records to pick out relevant evidence for prison instances. This expedites the discovery manner and improves the accuracy of evidence identification.

AI programs in regulation have the capability to enhance get proper of access to to justice for underserved populations who may also have restrained property to lease criminal illustration. Legal chatbots and on line sources provide reachable legal information and help.

AI models may be used to evaluate the chance of humans reoffending or failing to appear in court. This assists judges and probation officials in making statistics-pushed picks whilst considering the concepts of equity and justice.

AI technologies are instrumental in detecting and stopping cybercrime and fraud. AI-powered cybersecurity equipment can swiftly take a look at community facts to select out anomalies and ability protection breaches.

Artificial intelligence is transforming law and justice systems, empowering legal experts with higher studies skills, advanced decision-making device, and streamlined workflows. AI's predictive analytics and settlement assessment skills make a contribution to greater informed legal techniques and efficient contract control. Legal chatbots amplify access to justice, presenting essential records and assist to human beings on the lookout for crook assist. In crook justice, AI's risk evaluation and sentencing assist can foster extra normal and fair effects. Additionally, AI plays a crucial feature in preventing cybercrime and making sure facts safety in the legal area. As AI maintains to reinforce, it'll certainly revolutionize the criminal panorama, making justice extra accessible, green, and equitable for all. However, careful attention should receive to moral concerns and capability biases in AI structures to make sure that the generation is leveraged responsibly and with a dedication to equity and justice.

5.3.2 Perspectives on Social Equality and Justice Implications of Artificial Intelligence

The fast development of artificial intelligence (AI) brings every satisfaction and apprehension about its functionality effect on social equality and justice. As AI technologies emerge as more incorporated into numerous elements of society, it's miles vital to significantly have a study their implications for marginalized groups and inclined populations.

AI structures trained on biased statistics can perpetuate societal inequalities and discrimination. If historical data reflects biases, AI algorithms may inadvertently produce biased results in diverse domain names, collectively with hiring, lending, and crook justice.

AI's deployment can exacerbate gift social disparities, as people with more get right of entry to to AI era and resources might in all likelihood acquire more benefits. The digital divide and unequal access to AI device should deepen disparities in education, healthcare, and financial opportunities.

The lack of range among AI developers and researchers can motive biased algorithmic selection-making. To address this, greater diverse views and example in AI development groups are critical.

AI in surveillance, law enforcement, and social welfare increases ethical issues about privacy, human rights, and surveillance practices. Ensuring that AI is ethically deployed and aligned with social values is vital to shield justice.

AI's transformative capacity can disrupt conventional employment styles, possibly leading to method displacement for certain professions. Reskilling and upskilling obligations are important to equip humans for destiny mission possibilities.

On the excellent component, AI can enhance selection-making in justice systems, essential to extra equitable results. By analyzing big datasets, AI can help in figuring out kinds of bias and informing insurance modifications to sell social equality.

AI-powered legal chatbots and online resources can decorate get right of entry to to justice for underserved populations, imparting prison information and steerage to people who can't have enough cash legal instance.

AI's capability to analyze big datasets can provide policymakers with insights into social issues and tell proof-primarily based policy selections. This data-driven approach can reason more effective and equitable social packages.

Researchers are actively operating on developing AI algorithms that mitigate bias and promote fairness. Techniques like adverse schooling and fairness-conscious getting to know goal to cope with discriminatory consequences.

The status quo of sturdy AI governance frameworks, in conjunction with ethical tips, transparency, and accountability, is essential to ensure that AI serves societal dreams and values, selling social equality and justice.

Artificial intelligence holds mammoth functionality to form the destiny of society, and its effect on social equality and justice is multifaceted. While there are issues approximately bias, discrimination, and the amplification of inequalities, there are also possibilities for excessive satisfactory exchange. Responsible AI development, diversity in AI groups, and moral considerations can mitigate terrible implications and enhance the capability for AI to foster social justice. Emphasizing transparency, fairness, and inclusivity in AI deployment is crucial to make certain that AI generation make contributions to a extra equitable and clearly society, benefitting all individuals, irrespective of their records or instances. It is through thoughtful and conscientious adoption of AI that we can harness its strength to deal with societal challenges and create a more inclusive and equitable worldwide.

CHAPTER 6

Artificial Intelligence and Healthcare

6.1 The Use of Artificial Intelligence in Medicine and Healthcare

6.1.1 Artificial Intelligence Applications in Disease Diagnosis and Treatment

Artificial Intelligence (AI) has emerged as a recreation-changer inside the area of healthcare, specifically in sickness diagnosis and treatment. Its potential to investigate substantial amounts of information, understand styles, and make predictions has revolutionized medical practices, leading to greater correct and well timed diagnoses and customized treatment plans. Here, we delve into the various packages of AI in disease analysis and treatment:

AI-powered algorithms can examine clinical images, together with X-rays, MRIs, and CT scans, with top notch accuracy. AI structures can find out abnormalities, help in early detection of ailments like cancer, and guide radiologists in making more knowledgeable picks.

AI models can anticipate an person's hazard of developing nice ailments primarily based on their medical records, genetic information, and way of life factors. This early hazard assessment enables centered interventions and preventive measures.

AI can have a look at a affected character's medical information and remedy responses to indicate customized remedy plans. This tailored approach debts for character versions, optimizing remedy effectiveness.

AI speeds up drug discovery through reading huge datasets and simulating drug interactions. It identifies potential drug applicants, shortening the time and fee required for drug development.

AI-driven virtual health assistants offer customized scientific records, reminders, and treatment control to patients, enhancing healthcare accessibility and adherence.

AI algorithms beneficial useful resource pathologists in analyzing tissue samples and figuring out cell abnormalities, enhancing diagnostic accuracy and rushing up analysis.

AI-powered tracking systems constantly analyze affected person records to stumble on early symptoms and signs of deterioration, permitting timely interventions and reducing the chance of vital conditions.

AI gives medical choice help through way of synthesizing affected individual information and medical literature, helping physicians in making proof-based totally absolutely choices.

AI-pushed natural language processing techniques extract relevant facts from EHRs, making affected person records more to be had and facilitating studies and evaluation.

AI permits far flung affected individual monitoring thru wearable devices and sensors, permitting healthcare organizations to music patients' fitness in real-time and interfere proactively.

AI analyzes genomic statistics to identify genetic editions associated with illnesses, guiding precision medicine tactics for tailored remedies.

AI can prioritize patient triage in emergency conditions, optimizing useful resource allocation and streamlining affected person care.

AI optimizes clinical trial layout, identifying suitable affected character populations and predicting remedy responses, in the long run accelerating the drug development way.

AI-powered algorithms can encounter outbreaks of infectious ailments through reading facts from numerous sources, assisting public fitness authorities reply successfully.

AI analyzes imaging facts to extract quantitative features and find out genetic markers associated with diseases, facilitating customized treatment plans.

Artificial intelligence has ushered in a new era of opportunities in ailment prognosis and remedy. Its potential to approach and take a look at huge amounts of clinical facts, at the facet of its potential for custom designed care, has converted the healthcare landscape. From scientific imaging evaluation to drug discovery, AI's contributions are shaping the destiny of drugs, improving diagnostic accuracy, optimizing remedy techniques, and enhancing patient effects. As AI continues to adapt, it'll play an increasingly more crucial function in revolutionizing healthcare practices, making them greater green, on hand, and patient-centric. However, it is essential to cope with moral and regulatory troubles, ensuring that AI is deployed responsibly and in alignment with affected person privacy and protection.

6.1.2 Artificial Intelligence-Assisted Surgery and Medical Imaging

Artificial intelligence (AI) has considerably impacted the sphere of healthcare, particularly in surgical operation and scientific imaging. AI's integration into surgical techniques and medical imaging analysis has revolutionized scientific practices, improving surgical precision, diagnostic accuracy, and affected person outcomes.

AI has emerged as a treasured device in supporting surgeons at some stage in complex techniques. Using AI-powered robot structures, surgeons can attain more potent dexterity and precision, enabling minimally invasive surgical methods with smaller incisions and reduced patient trauma. The real-time comments supplied via manner of AI systems assists surgeons in making vital choices all through surgery, making sure more protection and successful results. Additionally, AI algorithms can analyze preoperative and intraoperative information, helping in surgical making plans and predicting capacity complications.

AI has revolutionized clinical imaging evaluation through supplying correct and green interpretations of severa imaging modalities. AI algorithms can quick have a look at scientific pics, including X-rays, MRIs, and CT scans, detecting abnormalities and assisting radiologists in diagnosing sicknesses. The speedy assessment of scientific snap shots hurries up the diagnostic manner, permitting well timed interventions and treatment making plans. AI also facilitates in identifying subtle styles and functions that might move ignored by means of way of the human eye, improving diagnostic accuracy and reducing the risk of misdiagnoses.

The integration of AI with medical imaging has in addition prolonged its talents in ailment analysis and remedy making plans. AI algorithms can examine complex imaging records and extract quantitative functions, assisting in the identification of precise disease markers and remedy goals. This approach, known as radiomics and radiogenomics, permits personalised treatment plans tailored to man or woman sufferers' dreams. Additionally, AI-powered clinical imaging can contribute to the early detection of sicknesses like cancer, contemplating timely interventions and improved affected person outcomes.

The destiny implications of AI-assisted surgery and medical imaging are promising. As AI algorithms maintain to evolve, they're predicted to emerge as greater state-of-the-art, further enhancing surgical precision and diagnostic accuracy.

AI's capability to research tremendous datasets and find out diffused styles ought to result in groundbreaking discoveries in sickness research and drug improvement. Moreover, AI-powered clinical imaging could rework the manner clinical professionals interpret images, improving healthcare accessibility and pleasant.

Despite its severa blessings, AI adoption in surgery and medical imaging additionally gives disturbing situations and moral concerns. Ensuring the safety and reliability of AI algorithms is paramount, as incorrect diagnoses or surgical choices may also want to have excessive consequences for patients. Moreover, retaining affected individual privateness and information protection within the context of AI-generated clinical records requires robust safeguards and adherence to information protection rules.

AI-assisted surgical treatment and medical imaging constitute a paradigm shift in healthcare. AI's ability to enhance surgical precision, enhance diagnostic accuracy, and help personalized remedy plans holds awesome promise for the future of medication. By addressing disturbing conditions and ethical issues, the accountable integration of AI in healthcare can unencumber its complete capability, reaping blessings patients and medical experts alike. As era continues to conform, AI's function in surgical remedy and medical imaging is poised to similarly increase healthcare practices, ushering in a modern day generation of precision medicine and advanced patient care.

6.2 Artificial Intelligence's Role in Drug Discovery and Hospital Management

6.2.1 Innovations in Drug Development via Artificial Intelligence

Artificial intelligence (AI) is revolutionizing the arena of drug development, providing novel answers to reinforce up the discovery and layout of latest pharmaceutical compounds. By leveraging machine getting to know algorithms and predictive modeling, AI has transformed conventional drug improvement processes, making them extra efficient and value-powerful.

AI plays a important position in drug discovery via reading big portions of biological and chemical facts. Through AI-pushed virtual screening, capability drug applicants can be recognized from large chemical libraries, narrowing down the look for promising compounds. AI algorithms are looking forward to the binding affinity of molecules to specific drug goals, notably dashing up the early ranges of drug discovery.

AI permits customized medicinal drug thru reading genomic statistics and identifying genetic markers associated with precise illnesses. This allows for the improvement of centered recovery tactics tailor-made to character patients' particular genetic profiles. AI's potential to count on treatment responses primarily based on genetic statistics complements the efficacy of drugs and decreases the threat of damaging reactions.

AI algorithms are hired to pick out out capability new makes use of for present pills, a manner known as drug repurposing. By analyzing drug databases and molecular structures, AI can endorse alternative therapeutic applications for tablets already authorized for specific conditions. Drug repurposing expedites the course to scientific trials and reduces the time and assets required for drug development.

AI optimizes scientific trial layout thru figuring out suitable affected character populations and predicting treatment responses. By reading affected person records and clinical literature, AI assists researchers in recruiting appropriate people and improving trial overall performance. AI can also understand functionality safety worries for the duration of trials, making sure affected person safety and facilitating faster drug approval.

The traditional drug improvement method is time-eating and luxurious. AI-driven approaches significantly reduce the time and fee required to understand capability drug applicants and optimize their efficacy. By streamlining early-level research and eliminating lots much less promising applicants early on, AI minimizes aid wastage and accelerates the route to a success drug improvement.

AI enables pick out capability protection troubles related to new drug candidates in advance than they input scientific trials. AI algorithms analyze statistics from preclinical research, animal fashions, and relevant databases to are watching for feasible damaging effects and protection dangers. This proactive method complements drug protection and decreases the chance of unexpected protection worries for the duration of human trials.

AI fosters collaboration among researchers and pharmaceutical groups by means of way of facilitating information sharing and integration. Through shared databases and AI-pushed platforms, researchers can access a wealth of facts, enhancing collective knowledge and accelerating drug discovery efforts.

The future implications of AI in drug improvement are considerable. As AI technology preserve to reinforce, they preserve the potential to discover progressive remedies for complex sicknesses that have eluded traditional techniques. Moreover, AI's integration with different current technology, along with nanotechnology and gene enhancing, can open new avenues for centered drug transport and gene recuperation tactics.

AI is reworking the landscape of drug development, presenting innovative answers to become aware of and format new pharmaceutical compounds. From AI-powered drug discovery to personalized treatment and repurposing present drugs, AI's applications are numerous and some distance-accomplishing. By accelerating medical trials, decreasing drug development costs, and improving drug safety, AI-pushed drug development is poised to revolutionize healthcare and bring transformative remedies to sufferers global. As researchers and pharmaceutical agencies keep to harness the electricity of AI, the destiny of drug improvement holds interesting opportunities for advanced patient results and the advancement of scientific generation.

6.2.2 Enhancing Hospital Efficiency and Route Optimization

Artificial intelligence (AI) is gambling a pivotal characteristic in improving sanatorium performance and optimizing diverse healthcare strategies. By leveraging AI algorithms and facts analytics, hospitals can streamline operations, improve affected person care, and optimize useful resource allocation.

AI-powered affected person triage structures analyze patient information and symptoms to prioritize instances primarily based mostly on severity. By rapid identifying critical times, healthcare companies can allocate sources and interest greater successfully, ensuring nicely timed treatment for the ones in want.

AI can automate appointment scheduling primarily based on affected individual options, healthcare issuer availability, and medical urgency. This reduces administrative burden and optimizes the allocation of medical team of workers's time, main to more green use of resources.

AI-driven mattress control structures are looking ahead to affected individual discharges, admission prices, and bed availability. This permits hospitals to proactively plan for affected individual go with the flow, lowering wait times and maximizing bed occupancy rates.

AI algorithms can optimize the routes for sanatorium body of workers, which incorporates nurses and physicians, to minimize tour time amongst affected person rooms and departments. This streamlines workflow and lets in healthcare providers to spend extra time on patient care.

AI analyzes historical data to are waiting for clinical gadget and supply needs, permitting hospitals to optimize stock manipulate. By making sure the availability of crucial resources, hospitals can keep away from shortages and decrease wastage.

AI-powered predictive protection can forecast machine disasters earlier than they occur, allowing proactive safety and decreasing downtime. This technique improves the durability of clinical device and enhances health center efficiency.

AI can look at virtual health information (EHRs) to become aware of styles and trends in affected character data. This assists healthcare carriers in making information-pushed selections, leading to higher patient outcomes and greater green treatment plans.

AI can constantly monitor affected person vitals and encounter anomalies in real-time, producing signals for scientific workforce in case of emergencies. This immediately response machine improves affected character safety and decreases the risk of damaging activities.

AI-pushed predictive analytics can forecast affected person admission quotes, affected person acuity, and useful resource necessities. This records-pushed approach enables sanatorium directors make knowledgeable decisions regarding staffing and useful resource allocation.

AI can automate billing methods, lowering errors and processing instances. This improves income cycle manipulate, ensuring properly timed reimbursements and monetary balance for hospitals.

Artificial intelligence is reworking clinic operations and healthcare manage through greater positive performance and optimized beneficial aid usage. AI-driven affected character triage, appointment scheduling, and mattress control streamline patient care delivery and decrease waiting instances. Optimized routes for sanatorium frame of workers and predictive maintenance of clinical tool improve workflow and gadget durability. AI's function in inventory control, EHR analysis, and real-time monitoring complements universal hospital performance and affected person safety. By leveraging AI for predictive analytics and automated billing, hospitals ought to make records-pushed selections and make certain easy revenue cycle manipulate. As AI keeps to decorate, its programs in healthcare are poised to make a profound effect on sanatorium operations, affected man or woman care, and the general healthcare panorama.

CHAPTER 7

Education and Artificial Intelligence

7.1 The Use of Artificial Intelligence in Education and Its Impact on Student Success

7.1.1 Personalized Education and Student Monitoring Systems

Artificial intelligence (AI) is revolutionizing the education quarter through presenting personalised mastering research and green pupil monitoring systems. Through AI-powered device and analytics, educators can cater to character scholar needs, tune development, and provide targeted help.

AI-pushed adaptive getting to know structures analyze university students' strengths, weaknesses, and analyzing patterns to tailor custom designed gaining knowledge of pathways. By imparting customized content and pacing, university college students can progress at their personal pace, enhancing engagement and information retention.

AI algorithms can take a look at university college students' academic overall performance and alternatives to deliver content material that aligns with their pursuits and abilties. This individualized method fosters a deeper knowledge of the problem depend and promotes lively getting to know.

Student tracking systems powered via AI can discover early signs and symptoms of tutorial struggles or disengagement. This permits educators to interfere right away and offer focused remediation, stopping studying gaps from widening.

AI-primarily based evaluation tools can generate customized quizzes and assignments, enabling continuous evaluation. Real-time comments facilitates college college students recognize their development and regions for development, promoting a increase attitude.

AI-powered studying structures can adapt to satisfy the specific desires of university college students with gaining knowledge of disabilities or particular educational necessities. Personalized interventions and inns foster inclusivity and accessibility in education.

AI analytics can count on student performance developments based totally on historical records and behavior patterns. Educators can use this information to understand university students at risk of falling at the back of and enforce interventions to make certain their success.

AI-powered pupil monitoring structures help optimize aid allocation by identifying regions of immoderate name for or unique educational needs. This permits academic institutions to allocate belongings strategically for maximum effect.

AI can assist teachers in refining their academic practices through customized professional improvement hints. AI-driven insights can assist educators decorate their training methodologies and stay up to date with first-rate practices.

AI algorithms can understand talented and proficient college students by using analyzing their instructional overall performance and capability. This allows educators to nurture and task those students correctly.

AI-based educational systems can propose supplementary sources, guides, and mastering substances to university students based on their hobbies and aspirations. This encourages a tradition of non-prevent getting to know past the classroom.

Personalized schooling and pupil monitoring systems powered by way of AI have the capability to convert the education panorama. By tailoring mastering tales to individual college students' goals and picks, AI fosters engagement, motivation, and educational success. Early intervention and adaptive guide systems make sure that no pupil is left in the back of, selling inclusivity and equity in training. Predictive analytics empower educators to make information-pushed picks, optimizing resource allocation and supplying centered interventions. AI's role in non-stop evaluation, custom designed comments, and teacher professional development complements coaching practices and student outcomes. As AI continues to adapt, its packages in training are poised to create a more effective, inclusive, and pupil-focused studying environment, making ready university college students for success in an ever-changing international.

7.1.2 Artificial Intelligence in Exams and Assessment Processes

Artificial intelligence (AI) is transforming the landscape of assessments and assessment tactics, revolutionizing the manner college students are evaluated and providing educators with powerful equipment to enhance the effectiveness and performance of assessments. From computerized grading to advanced analytics, AI's applications are reshaping the educational assessment paradigm.

AI-powered grading structures can mechanically observe more than one-desire questions, quick solutions, or even essays. By using herbal language processing and machine gaining knowledge of algorithms, AI as it should be and effectively assesses pupil responses, saving educators valuable time and decreasing grading mistakes.

AI permits immediately feedback to college students after finishing an evaluation. This actual-time feedback allows students to discover their errors and misconceptions immediately, encouraging a deeper information of the material and promoting a growth mindset.

AI can tailor checks to individual university college students' expertise ranges and reading styles. Adaptive evaluation systems alter the problem and content material based on university students' responses, making sure that every pupil's abilties are correctly measured.

AI-generated analytics offer educators with treasured insights into pupil general overall performance and development. Educators can perceive trends, music gaining knowledge of effects, and look into the effectiveness of educational techniques, permitting facts-pushed selection-making.

AI-powered plagiarism detection device can experiment and observe college students' written art work to grow to be privy to times of plagiarism. This helps keep academic integrity and encourages originality in university students' submissions.

AI analytics can count on college students' performance on destiny tests based totally on their historic facts and learning styles. This assists educators in expertise individual pupil wishes and designing targeted interventions for development.

AI can help reduce bias in assessments with the aid of using standardized and goal standards for grading. This guarantees fair evaluation and minimizes the have an effect on of subjective elements in the assessment machine.

AI technology can bolster examination safety with the resource of detecting and preventing cheating behaviors. Facial recognition and behavioral analysis can make sure that the right pupil is taking the exam and that the examination surroundings stays secure.

AI permits non-stop assessment, permitting educators to show college college students' improvement in some unspecified time in the future of the gaining knowledge of system. Regular checks provide a comprehensive data of students' strengths and weaknesses, allowing properly timed interventions.

AI streamlines examination management via automating various techniques, inclusive of examination scheduling, proctoring, and end result technology. This reduces administrative burdens and allows educators to awareness more on coaching and studying.

Artificial intelligence's integration into checks and evaluation tactics has converted how students are evaluated and the way educators leverage statistics to enhance teaching and studying. Automated grading and straight away comments beautify the performance and effectiveness of tests. AI's adaptability and personalization make sure that assessments align with person student needs and competencies. Advanced analytics empower educators with treasured insights, permitting information-driven decision-making and targeted interventions. By reducing bias, enhancing protection, and promoting continuous assessment, AI fosters trustworthy, dependable, and complete reviews. As AI keeps to enhance, its programs in academic checks will play an increasingly more essential characteristic in selling a greater inclusive, personalised, and facts-informed method to education.

7.2 Synergy Between Teachers and Artificial Intelligence

7.2.1 The Role of Artificial Intelligence in Educator Support and Tools

Artificial intelligence (AI) is revolutionizing the field of education via providing precious aid to educators and providing revolutionary gear to decorate training practices. From personalised lesson making plans to practical tutoring systems, AI's packages are transforming the manner educators supply coaching and useful resource student learning.

AI-powered equipment can have a look at scholar records, learning opportunities, and educational development to create personalised lesson plans for each student. Educators can tailor instructional content material and sports to deal with character studying needs, making sure a extra attractive and powerful mastering enjoy.

AI assists educators in producing educational content material, which incorporates quizzes, worksheets, and interactive studying substances. These AI-generated property align with curriculum requirements and cater to severa analyzing patterns, saving educators effort and time in content material creation.

AI-primarily based tutoring systems provide customized help to college college students, guiding them thru hard concepts and providing on the spot comments. Educators can screen college students' improvement and understand regions in which additional resource can be required.

AI analytics offer educators valuable insights into pupil average performance, reading styles, and areas of development. Educators can use this data to make informed picks, optimize teaching techniques, and implement focused interventions.

AI streamlines the grading method through automating the evaluation of assignments, quizzes, and checks. This saves educators time on repetitive obligations, permitting them to recognition extra on enticing with college students and imparting personalised comments.

AI-powered language learning gear can assist college college students in language acquisition via imparting interactive language lessons, pronunciation assist, and translation help. These equipment make language mastering greater on hand and attractive for college kids.

AI allows digital classrooms and collaborative reading environments, permitting educators to have interaction with college students in actual-time, regardless of their bodily place. AI-supported verbal exchange tools enhance on-line gaining knowledge of studies.

AI gadget can automate various administrative duties, together with scheduling, attendance monitoring, and report-retaining. This reduces administrative burdens on educators, permitting them to allocate extra time to training and scholar help.

AI offers personalised expert improvement recommendations based totally on educators' strengths and areas for development. This allows educators continuously beautify their coaching talents and stay up to date with the trendy academic practices.

AI-powered student support systems can become aware of college students who may additionally additionally want additional help and recommend suitable interventions. Educators can cope with students' social-emotional goals and academic disturbing situations greater correctly.

AI-primarily based speech reputation tools assist educators in transcribing and analyzing pupil responses in the course of beauty discussions and shows. These tools facilitate formative assessment and permit educators to song students' oral conversation skills.

AI-driven adaptive learning systems offer students custom designed getting to know pathways based on their performance and learning improvement. Educators can display student engagement and performance thru the platform's analytics.

The position of synthetic intelligence in educator assist and tools is transformative, offering a large kind of benefits to each educators and college students. AI allows personalised lesson making plans, content material introduction, and tutoring manual, fostering more individualized and powerful getting to know studies. Educators should make statistics-driven selections, automate administrative duties, and receive customized professional improvement hints via AI-powered equipment. Virtual classrooms, language getting to know guide, and collaboration gear decorate academic accessibility and engagement. AI's programs empower educators to deliver brilliant training and offer focused manual to university students, in the long run fostering a greater efficient, inclusive, and cutting-edge instructional environment. As AI keeps to beautify, its ability to useful resource educators and improve coaching practices will play a critical function in shaping the destiny of training for generations to come back.

7.2.2 Training Educators for the Future with Artificial Intelligence

As artificial intelligence (AI) continues to convert the sector of training, it turns into increasingly essential to equip educators with the crucial know-how and abilties to leverage AI efficaciously of their teaching practices. Training educators for the future with AI involves a entire method that addresses each the mixture of AI device inside the school room and the improvement of educators' AI literacy.

Effective schooling in AI begins offevolved with building educators' knowledge of AI fundamentals. Educators need to understand the primary ideas, terminology, and capabilities of AI to make informed picks approximately integrating AI device into their coaching practices.

Training educators with a focal point on AI ethics is essential. Educators ought to be privy to the moral implications of the usage of AI in schooling, which include information privacy, bias, and equity issues. Understanding the ones moral concerns ensures accountable and equitable use of AI in the school room.

Practical, arms-on revel in is crucial for educators to benefit self assurance in the use of AI gear efficaciously. Training programs need to provide opportunities for educators to check with AI packages, together with adaptive studying structures and AI-driven evaluation tools.

AI schooling for educators need to be tailored to their specific needs and difficulty areas. Customized expert improvement packages make sure that educators acquire applicable and realistic education aligned with their coaching obligations.

Encouraging collaboration and peer learning amongst educators fosters a supportive environment for AI adoption. Educators can percent their reports, exchange quality practices, and together explore modern tactics to apply AI in schooling.

AI is based totally heavily on information analysis and interpretation. Educators want to expand records literacy skills to effectively make use of AI-generated analytics and insights to enhance coaching and customize learning research.

The subject of AI is constantly evolving, and educators ought to engage in continuous learning to stay updated with the modern AI trends in education. Access to assets, webinars, and expert studying communities can aid ongoing studying.

AI training for educators ought to embody guidance on integrating AI-related topics into the curriculum. Educators can discover AI as a topic of take a look at or incorporate AI-related initiatives and activities all through diverse topics.

Promoting a growth mindset among educators encourages them to include new generation, which encompass AI, as possibilities for professional growth. A increase thoughts-set fosters a willingness to check, learn from disasters, and constantly improve.

Collaboration with AI professionals and researchers can beautify educators' information of AI packages in education. Partnerships can facilitate workshops, studies tasks, and expertise sharing to help educators' AI integration efforts.

Identifying and nurturing AI champions among educators can help strain the adoption of AI in faculties. These educators can feature mentors and advocates, inspiring others to encompass AI as a transformative tool in education.

Training educators for the future with artificial intelligence is a critical element of making sure a success AI integration in training. Equipping educators with AI literacy, realistic enjoy with AI system, and an statistics of AI ethics prepares them to successfully leverage AI to decorate training and scholar learning. Customized professional development, collaboration possibilities, and ongoing getting to know guide educators' adventure in the course of becoming gifted AI clients. By cultivating a growth attitude and embracing AI as a tool for innovation, educators can harness the functionality of AI to create attractive, custom designed, and destiny-equipped mastering opinions for university youngsters. As AI continues to reshape training, empowering educators with AI schooling will play a pivotal function in shaping the destiny of coaching and mastering for generations to return.

CHAPTER 8

Artificial Intelligence and Art

8.1 The Use of Artificial Intelligence in Art and Its Contributions to Creative Processes

8.1.1 Artificial Intelligence-Generated Art and Cultural Identity

Artificial intelligence (AI) has spread out new opportunities within the global of paintings, which incorporates the advent of AI-generated works of art. These computer-generated inventive endeavors have sparked discussions about the intersection of AI, creativity, and cultural identity.

AI-generated artwork involves using algorithms and gadget learning techniques to provide seen or auditory creations. Some AI systems are able to analyzing considerable amounts of current artwork after which generating new portions based totally on located styles and patterns. This raises questions about the nature of creativity and whether AI can absolutely be taken into consideration creative in the identical manner as human artists.

Art has lengthy been taken into consideration an expression of cultural identity. Human artists regularly draw notion from their cultural backgrounds, facts, and reviews, reflecting their specific identities of their artwork. With AI-generated art work, the query arises: Can machines capture and express cultural identification within the equal way as human artists?

One software of AI in artwork is to replicate the kinds of famous artists from special cultures and time periods. AI algorithms can take a look at an artist's body of work and create new pieces that mimic their creative style. While this may be mind-blowing from a technical perspective, it increases concerns approximately authenticity and originality.

AI-generated artwork that draws concept from particular cultural traditions can likely cause troubles of cultural appropriation. As AI systems examine from present art work, there's a hazard of reproducing cultural elements with out a deep expertise in their significance and context, main to misrepresentations or insensitive portrayals.

AI-generated art work blurs the bounds between human and device creativity. Some argue that AI artwork represents a new form of creative expression, outstanding from human art, while others view it as an extension of human creativity. The debate over the distinction among human and AI artwork stays an ongoing communique within the paintings global.

Rather than replacing human artists, AI may be visible as a tool that artists can use to beautify their modern approach. Some artists collaborate with AI systems, the usage of them as assistants or assets of idea, combining human vision and expression with the talents of AI algorithms.

As AI paintings will become extra everyday, moral considerations come to the forefront. Issues of authorship, ownership, and copyright are complex with reference to AI-generated art. Determining the criminal and moral frameworks surrounding AI artwork stays a mission.

AI-generated paintings offers a charming exploration of the connection among technology, creativity, and cultural identity. As AI maintains to boost, it will increase profound questions about the character of artwork, the placement of artists, and the maintenance of cultural identity in a technologically driven worldwide. While AI has tested first rate abilties in replicating innovative patterns, it additionally prompts vital discussions about authenticity, cultural appropriation, and the evolving landscape of artwork. The intersection of AI and cultural identification in artwork remains an evolving and belief-scary subject matter that requires ongoing attention and communicate within the art network and society at massive.

8.1.2 The Collaboration Between Artists and Artificial Intelligence within the Future

The future holds first rate capacity for collaboration among artists and artificial intelligence (AI), ushering in a present day generation of creativity and innovation inside the artwork international. As AI technologies preserve to enhance, artists are exploring strategies to harness AI as a effective tool and medium for artistic expression.

In the destiny, AI is expected to serve as a innovative associate for artists in place of a replacement. Artists can use

AI algorithms to generate thoughts, discover new resourceful patterns, and push the boundaries of their creativity. AI can offer sparkling views and idea, sparking novel thoughts that artists won't have considered on their private.

AI's vast computational abilities allow artists to discover new inventive opportunities that have been formerly impossible. AI can machine large portions of data, generate complex visualizations, and create complicated patterns, establishing doorways to innovative artwork bureaucracy and testimonies.

The collaboration between artists and AI might be to result in the emergence of hybrid artwork forms that mix human creativity with AI-driven factors. These new paintings forms might also additionally integrate conventional artwork strategies with AI-generated content material material, growing precise and immersive innovative studies.

AI's capability to research and interpret information can result in the advent of personalized and interactive artistic endeavors. Artists can use AI algorithms to tailor creative endeavors based on character alternatives, feelings, or opinions, offering visitors a more appealing and personalized art come across.

AI-powered paintings collaborations have the capacity to address vital societal demanding situations and activate meaningful conversations. Artists can use AI to visualize complex data units related to issues like climate change, social inequalities, or health crises, making these topics extra accessible and engaging for the public.

Collaborating with AI increases ethical questions and conceptual explorations for artists. Artists may delve into the problem subjects of AI's impact on society, the blurring of limitations among human and system creativity, and the perception of authorship and possession in AI-generated art work.

AI can make a contribution to the safety of ingenious traditions and cultural historic beyond. By analyzing and replicating paintings from unique cultures and ancient durations, AI can help keep and promote diverse artistic practices for future generations.

The collaboration among artists and AI also can extend to art work training. AI may be used to increase customized artwork gaining knowledge of evaluations, offer remarks on pupil artwork, and offer gadget for exploring diverse creative techniques and styles.

AI can use art as a medium to communicate its very very own information and interpretations of the sector. AI-generated artwork can be a manner for AI systems to specific their knowledge, notion, and emotional responses, supplying particular insights into the inner workings of AI.

The collaboration among artists and synthetic intelligence promises a dynamic and transformative future for the artwork international. As AI technology enhance, artists have the opportunity to discover new innovative possibilities, create hybrid artwork paperwork, and deal with urgent societal worrying conditions. AI can function a innovative companion, empowering artists to push the limits in their creativity and offer personalized and interactive artwork reports. The moral and conceptual dimensions of AI-art collaborations will remain crucial areas of exploration, as artists navigate questions of authorship, authenticity, and the evolving position of AI inside the innovative process. The future collaboration among artists and AI holds thrilling ability for reshaping artwork, generation, and the human revel in.

CHAPTER 9

Security and Privacy

9.1 Threats to Security Posed through Artificial Intelligence and Defense Mechanisms

9.1.1 Artificial Intelligence-Driven Cyber Attacks and Countermeasures

The rapid advancement of synthetic intelligence (AI) has now not best delivered about numerous blessings but has also supplied new demanding situations inside the realm of cybersecurity. As AI generation grow to be extra cutting-edge, cyber attackers are leveraging AI-driven strategies to release more complicated and focused cyber assaults. In reaction, cybersecurity professionals and groups are growing revolutionary countermeasures to protect toward those evolving threats.

AI-powered malware and phishing attacks have come to be more contemporary and tough to hit upon. AI can observe vast amounts of records to craft convincing phishing emails or install malware that could adapt its conduct to avoid traditional protection features.

AI allows cyber attackers to release APTs that stay undetected for extended durations. AI-pushed APTs can autonomously check out a goal's vulnerabilities, select out suitable assault vectors, and hide malicious activities, making them exceedingly continual and tough to counter.

AI algorithms can be used to automate brute pressure assaults on passwords and encryption keys. AI-pushed attacks can intelligently guess passwords primarily based on styles and common phrases, probably compromising touchy facts.

AI-generated deepfake content fabric can be used for disinformation campaigns, spreading fake narratives or manipulating public opinion. Such assaults have extensive implications for political and social balance.

AI-powered cyber attacks can live far from conventional detection structures via mimicking legitimate person behavior, making them hard to distinguish from normal sports. This allows attackers to live undetected for extended periods.

Cybersecurity professionals are harnessing AI to enhance threat detection talents. AI-driven anomaly detection systems can pick out out uncommon styles and behaviors indicative of cyber attacks, permitting speedy responses.

By leveraging AI-pushed behavioral biometrics, corporations can constantly display user interactions to grow to be aware about anomalies and capability protection threats based totally on individual conduct.

AI-pushed endpoint protection solutions can hit upon and block brand new malware and ransomware assaults in actual-time, safeguarding endpoints and critical systems.

To fight deepfake attacks, researchers are growing AI-based deepfake detection equipment that could emerge as aware about manipulated content material and distinguish it from proper media.

AI-powered incident response gear can automate the evaluation and containment of cyber threats, reducing response times and minimizing the effect of assaults.

Sharing AI-pushed hazard intelligence at some stage in businesses and industries complements the collective ability to pick out out and reply to emerging cyber threats efficaciously.

Combining human know-how with AI-pushed gear lets in protection experts to make extra informed choices and stay one step beforehand of AI-pushed attackers.

Raising recognition approximately AI-driven cyber threats amongst employees and cease-clients is essential. Security consciousness training enables customers recognize phishing attempts and different social engineering techniques.

Periodic safety audits and vulnerability exams assist companies become aware of and address ability weaknesses of their infrastructure, decreasing the attack ground for cybercriminals.

The upward push of AI-driven cyber assaults poses substantial traumatic situations for cybersecurity specialists and organizations global. However, the proactive deployment of AI-based definitely safety mechanisms and collaborative efforts can bolster cyber resilience and mitigate the impact of those threats. AI-driven chance detection, behavioral biometrics, and deepfake detection are just some of the countermeasures that show the functionality of AI in safeguarding in competition to growing cyber threats. As the cyber landscape keeps to evolve, ongoing research, improvement, and innovation may be crucial in staying earlier of AI-pushed cyber attackers and making sure a consistent digital surroundings for people and organizations.

9.1.2 Artificial Intelligence's Role in Defense and Security

Artificial intelligence (AI) is all of sudden remodeling the panorama of defense and protection, revolutionizing the manner military forces and safety corporations perform and respond to rising threats. The integration of AI era holds the promise of improving situational recognition, optimizing choice-making approaches, and improving typical protection abilities.

AI-driven structures can analyze tremendous quantities of records from various belongings, consisting of satellite tv for pc imagery, social media, and sensor networks, to discover capacity threats and collect critical intelligence. This permits real-time threat detection and early caution abilties, empowering protection and safety forces to proactively reply to safety disturbing situations.

AI plays a pivotal feature in growing self maintaining systems and robotics, allowing unmanned cars, drones, and robots to carry out a number of responsibilities, which include reconnaissance, surveillance, and logistics. Autonomous systems reduce the risks to human employees and provide more desirable project capabilities.

AI is essential in preventing cyber threats and securing essential networks and infrastructure. AI-powered cybersecurity equipment can rapidly stumble on and reply to cyberattacks, discover anomalies, and strengthen defenses closer to evolving threats like malware, ransomware, and superior continual threats (APTs).

AI algorithms can examine styles and dispositions in facts to are anticipating potential terrorist sports or discover styles of radicalization. This permits security groups to take preemptive moves and disrupt terrorist plots earlier than they can be completed.

AI enhances biometric identification and authentication methods, which include facial popularity, fingerprint scanning, and voice recognition. These technology provide a boost to get proper of access to govern measures and make a contribution to more suitable border protection and regulation enforcement efforts.

AI-driven predictive protection algorithms can anticipate gadget failures and optimize protection schedules, lowering downtime and improving the performance of protection system and assets.

AI-powered natural language processing (NLP) permits the automatic assessment of big amounts of textual information, together with open-supply intelligence, news articles, and reviews. This lets in intelligence analysts to extract treasured insights and investigate the sentiment or credibility of statistics.

AI assists army and security employees in making well-knowledgeable selections with the aid of imparting records-pushed insights and situation simulations. Decision guide structures enhance situational awareness and manual effective responses to dynamic and complicated conditions.

AI technologies, including computer imaginative and prescient and item detection, bolster border protection and surveillance efforts. AI-pushed surveillance systems can screen borders, ports, and vital infrastructure, identifying capability threats and unauthorized sports activities.

AI performs a important function in catastrophe reaction and humanitarian assist by means of the usage of facilitating rapid harm evaluation, resource allocation, and coordination of alleviation efforts. AI-powered drones and robots may be deployed to get right of entry to and determine hard-to-attain areas.

Artificial intelligence's role in protection and protection is transformative, empowering navy forces and protection organizations with superior abilities to deal with complicated and evolving demanding situations. From chance detection and intelligence analysis to cybersecurity, impartial systems, and predictive analytics, AI enhances the efficiency, effectiveness, and agility of protection and safety operations. As AI generation keep to comply, ongoing studies, improvement, and ethical issues are critical to make certain that AI is deployed responsibly and in alignment with international norms and human rights standards. Embracing the capacity of AI even as addressing its challenges can be important in harnessing the overall power of synthetic intelligence for the advantage of worldwide defense and protection efforts.

9.2 The Relationship Between Artificial Intelligence and Cybersecurity

9.2.1 Artificial Intelligence-Enhanced Cybersecurity Tools

In the ever-evolving landscape of cybersecurity threats, the mixing of synthetic intelligence (AI) has turn out to be a sport-changer. AI-improved cybersecurity equipment are remodeling how corporations come upon, save you, and reply to cyberattacks. These wise solutions leverage AI algorithms to analyze large portions of information, pick out patterns, and are watching for capability threats with unparalleled tempo and accuracy.

AI-powered cybersecurity gear excel at detecting advanced and previously unknown threats. By constantly tracking community website online visitors, device logs, and person behavior, those equipment can become aware about anomalous patterns that might imply malicious activity. This proactive technique allows corporations to cope with capability threats earlier than they're capable of reason big damage.

AI-pushed cybersecurity gear use behavioral assessment to create person profiles and perceive deviations from ordinary conduct. These gadget can locate unauthorized get admission to attempts, insider threats, and different suspicious sports activities primarily based on deviations from installed consumer patterns.

AI-powered cybersecurity tools offer real-time incident reaction skills. When a capability risk is detected, AI can trigger computerized responses, which incorporates blocking off suspicious IP addresses, separating compromised gadgets, or quarantining malware-inflamed files.

AI algorithms excel at figuring out new and evolving sorts of malware, at the side of polymorphic and 0-day threats. These tools can find malware based totally on behavioral trends and prevent its execution, even in advance than traditional signature-based totally antivirus solutions can update their databases.

AI-driven cybersecurity tools decorate defenses toward phishing attacks and social engineering techniques. AI can look at e mail content and sender behavior to find out phishing tries, stopping personnel from falling victim to fraudulent schemes.

AI-powered protection analytics can anticipate capability cyber threats based totally mostly on ancient statistics and modern-day-day trends. This predictive method permits organizations to allocate sources greater effectively, prioritize safety features, and proactively deal with rising threats.

AI-more suitable cybersecurity equipment can discover uncommon network sports, which includes port scanning, information exfiltration, or Distributed Denial of Service (DDoS) attacks. By reading community visitors in actual-time, AI can brief spot anomalies and trigger safety indicators.

AI algorithms can enhance endpoint protection through reading gadget behaviors and figuring out symptoms of compromise or unauthorized get proper of entry to. This level of endpoint monitoring ensures a better protection toward malware and unauthorized intrusions.

AI-driven cybersecurity gear can autonomously respond to low-degree safety incidents, relieving protection agencies from habitual duties. This allows human professionals to popularity on more complex and strategic cybersecurity demanding situations.

AI-greater suitable cybersecurity gadget continuously have a look at from new records and adapt their models to stay in advance of evolving threats. This self-gaining knowledge of capability permits AI to conform and enhance its detection and reaction abilties over time.

AI-extra appropriate cybersecurity gear have revolutionized the manner corporations shield their digital property and sensitive statistics. The integration of AI algorithms provides superior risk detection, actual-time incident reaction, and predictive protection analytics, permitting organizations to proactively guard in opposition to cyber threats. As cyberattacks become extra state-of-the-art, AI-driven solutions play a vital position in retaining tempo with the ever-changing chance landscape. By leveraging the energy of AI, agencies can bolster their cybersecurity posture, decorate their defense abilties, and live one step in advance of cyber adversaries. However, whilst AI offers superb ability in cybersecurity, it's miles critical to make certain accountable and moral use, consisting of addressing capacity biases and privateness problems. A balanced approach to AI integration, combined with the knowledge of professional cybersecurity professionals, may be key to developing a resilient and strong digital environment in the face of evolving cyber threats.

9.2.2 Data Security and Encryption with Artificial Intelligence

Data protection is a paramount undertaking for organizations and people alike in contemporary digital age. With the ever-developing quantity of records and the growing sophistication of cyber threats, the function of synthetic intelligence (AI) in information protection and encryption has turn out to be instrumental in safeguarding sensitive records. AI-pushed answers provide modern methods to beautify information safety, improve encryption strategies, and respond to rising safety challenges.

AI performs a critical function in identifying and mitigating capacity records safety threats. AI-driven chance detection solutions constantly examine network site visitors, customer conduct, and tool logs to understand styles indicative of cyber attacks or statistics breaches. This actual-time tracking allows prompt responses to security incidents.

AI algorithms can stumble on anomalies in facts get proper of entry to styles and user behavior, assisting to become aware of unauthorized access tries and insider threats. By organising baseline behavior, AI-stronger structures can speedy flag unusual activities, alerting protection agencies to capability protection risks.

AI-powered records protection analytics leverage gadget getting to know to predict ability protection breaches or vulnerabilities primarily based totally on historic statistics and rising trends. These predictive insights enable proactive measures to enhance statistics safety and prevent potential threats.

AI can decorate encryption key control, making sure the stable technology, distribution, and rotation of encryption keys. AI-driven structures can automate key control duties, decreasing human errors and improving the overall protection of encrypted records.

AI generation contribute to the improvement of extra robust encryption algorithms, making it increasingly tough for adversaries to crack encrypted statistics. AI can study modern encryption techniques, perceive weaknesses, and recommend enhancements for stronger information safety.

As quantum computing poses a functionality chance to traditional encryption strategies, AI may be used to broaden quantum-resistant encryption strategies. AI can assist in exploring placed up-quantum cryptography solutions that stay consistent even inside the face of quantum computing improvements.

AI can facilitate regular statistics get entry to and sharing via multi-element authentication and get entry to controls. AI-pushed systems can reveal information get proper of entry to styles and dynamically modify get right of access to privileges primarily based on consumer conduct and safety guidelines.

AI-powered DLP solutions assist prevent information leakage and unauthorized records transfers. By studying statistics utilization styles and content, AI can come to be privy to and block tries to exfiltrate sensitive statistics, decreasing the hazard of facts breaches.

AI can bolster endpoint protection via detecting and mitigating threats at the tool degree. AI-pushed endpoint protection answers screen gadget behaviors and understand signs and symptoms of compromise, supplying an extra layer of safety in the direction of cyber threats.

AI contributes to improving cloud protection by way of figuring out and addressing capability vulnerabilities in cloud environments. AI-driven cloud security solutions constantly inspect cloud configurations and activities to make sure records saved in the cloud remains blanketed.

Artificial intelligence is revolutionizing information protection and encryption practices, empowering organizations to defend their touchy information from ever-evolving cyber threats. From AI-powered danger detection and predictive analytics to advanced encryption algorithms and quantum-resistant cryptography, AI's contributions to statistics safety are profound. The integration of AI in statistics security features enhances the effectiveness of encryption strategies, strengthens facts get proper of access to controls, and lets in groups to respond hastily to protection incidents. However, as AI maintains to growth, it's far critical to cope with capability ethical issues and make certain accountable AI implementation in information safety practices. By harnessing the electricity of AI and mixing it with the understanding of cybersecurity specialists, groups can installation a sturdy and resilient records safety framework, safeguarding their valuable data in an more and more connected and digitized international.

CHAPTER 10

The Future of Artificial Intelligence

10.1 The Potential and Expected Developments of Artificial Intelligence in the Future

10.1.1 Predictions for the Future of Artificial Intelligence

As artificial intelligence (AI) maintains to improve abruptly, the future holds thrilling opportunities and ability alterations in the course of various industries and elements of human life. While it's far challenging to are watching for the perfect trajectory of AI improvement, specialists and researchers have diagnosed numerous tendencies and predictions that could shape the future of artificial intelligence.

Researchers intention to growth General AI, moreover referred to as Artificial General Intelligence (AGI), which refers to AI systems that personal human-like intelligence and capabilities. AGI could have the ability to recognize, take a look at, and carry out a considerable variety of duties at a human level, representing a enormous milestone in AI development.

AI-pushed automation is expected to revolutionize severa industries, predominant to elevated productiveness and performance. From production and logistics to healthcare and finance, AI-powered automation is probably to convert the manner we paintings and do business enterprise.

Advancements in NLP will bring about more sophisticated language information and verbal exchange among human beings and AI structures. This development will power the improvement of more superior digital assistants, chatbots, and language translation gear.

As AI will become extra pervasive, the focus on moral AI improvement will intensify. Efforts to make certain fairness, transparency, and obligation in AI algorithms and choice-making techniques turns into paramount to deal with potential biases and social implications.

AI is anticipated to play a vast function in revolutionizing healthcare and medication. AI-driven medical diagnostics, drug discovery, personalized remedy plans, and far off affected man or woman tracking are genuinely a number of the areas that preserve great promise in the future.

AI-generated art, song, and literature are anticipated to come to be greater trendy, blurring the traces among human and AI creativity. AI may also moreover even make contributions to collaborative art tasks, in which human artists paintings along AI systems to produce particular masterpieces.

AI is probable to play a vital role in personalised and adaptive analyzing evaluations, tailoring training to individual university college students' wishes and gaining knowledge of patterns. AI-driven tutoring systems and smart educational gear becomes extra time-venerated.

Advancements in AI technologies will accelerate the improvement and adoption of autonomous automobiles, reshaping the transportation industry. Self-riding cars and vans are expected to end up greater common on roads, revolutionizing mobility and logistics.

AI will more and more be used to reinforce human competencies, permitting people to perform responsibilities extra efficaciously and effectively. Human-AI collaboration turns into more normal in fields like remedy, engineering, and medical studies.

The development of quantum computing may also moreover cause breakthroughs in AI, unlocking new abilities and fixing complex issues at an extremely good scale. Quantum AI is expected to have a profound effect on numerous AI packages.

AI is probably to play a critical function in addressing weather change worrying conditions. AI-driven solutions can optimize power consumption, expect intense weather events, and help layout greater sustainable cities and infrastructure.

AI technology will useful resource space exploration missions, enabling self sustaining spacecraft, shrewd rovers, and advanced facts analysis for medical discoveries past Earth.

The destiny of synthetic intelligence holds super promise, with enhancements in AGI, extended automation, and breakthroughs in herbal language processing. Ethical troubles and accountable AI improvement will stay essential as AI will become increasingly more protected into our every day lives. AI's capability to revolutionize healthcare, education, transportation, and diverse other industries affords exciting possibilities for development and powerful societal impact. As AI era hold to conform, collaborative efforts among researchers, policymakers, and enterprise leaders can be critical in shaping the destiny of AI in a manner that blessings humanity and addresses potential demanding situations.

10.1.2 The Boundaries and Possible Directions of Artificial Intelligence

Artificial Intelligence (AI) has made extraordinary strides in cutting-edge years, but there are nonetheless easy barriers that form its cutting-edge capabilities. As we appearance to the future, numerous viable guidelines for AI improvement are rising.

Presently, AI is basically confined to Narrow AI, which refers to AI systems designed for particular duties, consisting of picture reputation or herbal language processing. General AI, but, may have human-like intelligence and versatility, however achieving it remains a huge task.

AI's improvement increases moral worries, along with bias in algorithms, privateness troubles, and the capability impact on employment. Ensuring that AI is advanced and deployed responsibly and ethically is essential to cope with the ones problems.

While AI can generate marvelous art work, tune, and literature, attaining actual human-stage creativity and emotional expertise remains an open question.

AI lacks recognition and self-recognition. The query of whether or not or not AI can growth actual focus or knowledge of its personal life stays a philosophical debate.

AI will keep to excel in slender domains, with ongoing upgrades in fields like natural language processing, computer imaginative and prescient, and robotics. These tendencies might also have profound implications for numerous industries, including healthcare, finance, and production.

The popularity on moral AI development will reinforce, with efforts to deal with biases, sell transparency, and set up suggestions for responsible AI use.

AI will increasingly paintings along people as collaborative partners, augmenting human competencies in severa fields. This partnership will result in greater efficient and powerful trouble-fixing.

There might be a growing call for for AI systems to offer factors for his or her decisions, in particular in important programs like healthcare and finance. Researchers will paintings on growing AI models that could provide obvious reasoning at the back of their outputs.

The marriage of AI and quantum computing also can open up new possibilities for fixing complex problems and optimizing AI algorithms.

Researchers will keep to pursue Artificial General Intelligence (AGI), which goals to create AI systems with human-like cognitive capabilities. However, undertaking AGI stays uncertain and can be a vast assignment for the future.

AI will likely play an more and more distinguished feature in vicinity exploration, assisting in self reliant spacecraft navigation, records analysis, and choice-making in far flung and difficult environments.

AI may be leveraged to deal with climate trade demanding situations, inclusive of optimizing power intake, predicting weather patterns, and assisting in climate modeling.

While AI has made mind-blowing strides, it is vital to apprehend the boundaries that currently shape its skills. Narrow AI dominates the sector, and achieving General AI and actual human-degree intelligence remain faraway desires. Ethical problems will guide AI development to make certain responsible and beneficial use. Looking earlier, AI will maintain to enhance in narrow domains, and human-AI collaboration becomes more everyday. Researchers will find out new frontiers including quantum AI and AGI, and AI's ability in region exploration and climate alternate answers can be harnessed for the benefit of humanity. As we navigate the future of AI, placing the right balance between technological improvement and ethical issues may be essential to form AI's effect on society in a exceptional and transformative way.

10.2 Challenges within the Relationship Between Humanity and Artificial Intelligence

10.2.1 The Role of Ethics and Its Importance within the Future

Ethics performs a pivotal characteristic in shaping the future of era, mainly in fields like synthetic intelligence (AI). As AI maintains to enhance and end up increasingly included into various elements of our lives, the ethical concerns surrounding its improvement, deployment, and use come to be more crucial than ever. The characteristic of ethics inside the destiny of AI is multifaceted, encompassing each the responsible development of AI technology and their effect on society.

Ethics publications the improvement of AI technology in a way that aligns with human values and respects character rights. Ethical AI improvement consists of addressing biases in AI algorithms, ensuring transparency in decision-making strategies, and selling equity and responsibility in AI systems.

Ethical concerns demand that AI programs are designed to keep away from harm to humans and society. Ensuring the protection and safety of AI systems is crucial, specifically in vital domains consisting of healthcare, self reliant vehicles, and cybersecurity.

AI often relies on large quantities of information, elevating worries approximately privateness and statistics protection. Ethical AI frameworks prioritize the safeguarding of private statistics and endorse for smooth consent mechanisms for data usage.

AI algorithms can inadvertently perpetuate biases present within the facts they are educated on, main to unfair outcomes. Ethical AI improvement includes actively mitigating biases and making sure fairness in AI preference-making, especially in applications like hiring, lending, and crook justice.

Ethical AI structures are designed to be transparent and provide causes for their decisions. Users ought so one can apprehend how AI arrived at a particular conclusion, mainly in critical contexts like healthcare analysis or mortgage approvals.

Ethics emphasizes the importance of human-AI collaboration, wherein AI serves as a device to beautify human talents in preference to replace them. Ethical AI development targets to empower people and decorate decision-making, in location of decreasing human autonomy.

Ethical AI considers the wider societal effect of AI technologies and advocates for inclusive development. It takes into account the numerous dreams of various groups and strives to create AI structures that gain all segments of society.

Ethics requires robust governance and regulation of AI generation to make certain responsible and accountable use. Policymakers and stakeholders need to art work collectively to installation frameworks that balance innovation and ethical issues.

Ethical AI improvement is an iterative method that involves non-stop evaluation and development. As AI technology evolve, ethical troubles ought to adapt to deal with new demanding situations and ability risks.

Ethical AI fosters accept as true with and acceptance among clients and stakeholders. When AI systems are advanced with moral standards in mind, people are more likely to include and adopt these technology.

Ethical problems help find out and deal with unintended outcomes of AI deployment, mitigating capacity bad influences on individuals and society.

By prioritizing ethics, AI improvement may be more sustainable and responsible, making sure that AI upgrades are in harmony with societal values and dreams.

Ethical AI improvement safeguards fundamental human rights, consisting of privateness, dignity, and autonomy, selling a human-centric method to era.

Ethical AI development contributes to the lengthy-time period viability of AI era. Addressing ethical demanding situations head-on permits AI to be a high fine stress for humanity over the lengthy haul.

Ethics performs a crucial feature in shaping the future of synthetic intelligence. Responsible AI improvement, protection, privateness, equity, and transparency are essential concerns to make certain AI technology advantage society even as minimizing potential harms. Emphasizing ethics in AI improvement is not definitely an ethical vital but additionally a strategic choice to assemble accept as true with, foster beauty, and create AI structures that really effect individuals and the broader society. As AI technologies keep to comply, a dedication to ethical ideas can be key in guiding AI's function in shaping a better, extra inclusive, and sustainable future for all.

10.2.2 Controlling and Being Responsible with Artificial Intelligence

As synthetic intelligence (AI) keeps to develop and integrate into diverse elements of our lives, it turns into critical to exert control and act responsibly in its development and deployment. The electricity and potential of AI convey each benefits and annoying situations, making responsible AI improvement critical to ensure its exceptional effect on society.

Establishing moral AI frameworks is paramount to manual the improvement and use of AI technologies. These frameworks must embody requirements in conjunction with equity, transparency, duty, privateness safety, and minimizing bias to ensure AI operates in alignment with human values and respects person rights.

AI systems have to be designed to provide transparent choice-making procedures. Users and stakeholders want to understand how AI arrives at its conclusions to don't forget and acquire its outputs. Explainable AI methodologies assist in offering clean causes for AI choices.

Maintaining human oversight and manage over AI systems is critical to prevent unintentional results and capability biases. While AI can automate obligations, people must remain inside the loop to validate effects, interpret context, and interfere when critical.

Governments and policymakers play a vital position in organising robust regulatory and jail frameworks for AI. These frameworks have to cope with problems which include statistics privacy, algorithmic responsibility, safety necessities, and legal responsibility to make sure accountable AI use.

AI algorithms need to go through rigorous sorting out and validation to become aware of and mitigate biases. Bias in AI structures can perpetuate modern-day inequalities and discrimination, so efforts to address these biases are important to make sure equity and inclusivity.

Controlling AI involves prioritizing protection and protection. AI systems have to be designed to locate and mitigate potential vulnerabilities and protect in opposition to adverse attacks.

AI technology have to be state of affairs to non-stop tracking and evaluation. Regular audits and tests assist pick out out capacity risks and demanding situations, taking into account essential upgrades and updates.

Stakeholders from numerous domain names, consisting of academia, industry, governments, and civil society, ought to collaborate to form the accountable improvement and use of AI. Such partnerships ensure a numerous range of views and information are taken into consideration.

Educating developers, users, and policymakers approximately accountable AI practices is essential. Raising recognition about moral AI thoughts and their application facilitates create a shared information of AI's potential and obstacles.

Being accountable with AI way considering its broader societal impact. Stakeholders must look into the ability implications of AI deployment on people, agencies, and numerous industries, ensuring that AI benefits society as an entire.

AI should be developed inclusively, taking into consideration numerous views and desires. Ensuring illustration from special businesses and demographics permits cope with biases and create AI structures that cater to all customers.

AI technologies need to be deployed responsibly, considering capacity dangers and blessings. A careful method is crucial, specially in immoderate-stakes applications together with healthcare, finance, and essential infrastructure.

Controlling and being accountable with synthetic intelligence is vital to harness its potential for the more proper.

Ethical AI frameworks, transparency, human oversight, and regulatory hints are essential components in shaping the destiny of AI. As AI generation retain to conform, collective efforts from stakeholders, coupled with ongoing studies and moral worries, can be key to ensuring AI's advantageous effect on society while mitigating ability risks and demanding situations. Responsible AI improvement and deployment pave the way for a future where AI technology paintings harmoniously with people, improving our abilties and improving our lives in a accountable and sustainable way.

10.3 Shaping the Future with Artificial Intelligence

10.3.1 The Societal, Economic, and Cultural Transformations Driven by using the use of Artificial Intelligence

Artificial Intelligence (AI) has emerged as a transformative pressure, using full-size modifications in numerous factors of society, the economy, and way of existence. As AI era hold to increase, their effect on the ones domains turns into greater referred to, shaping the arena we live in.

AI is reshaping the process marketplace by way of automating repetitive obligations and augmenting human talents. While it creates new undertaking possibilities in AI-related fields, it also increases concerns about task displacement and the want for upskilling and reskilling the body of people.

AI is revolutionizing healthcare with stepped forward diagnostics, customized remedy plans, and drug discovery. AI-pushed clinical gadgets and remote affected character tracking structures are enhancing affected individual consequences and accessibility to brilliant healthcare.

AI is remodeling education thru customized studying stories, adaptive tutoring, and clever educational equipment. It permits educators to tailor training to person pupil needs, fostering better mastering effects.

AI is being used to decorate social services like welfare distribution, resource allocation, and catastrophe response. AI-pushed analytics assist governments and organizations make information-driven choices for additonal efficient provider transport.

AI brings ethical demanding situations, which includes algorithmic biases, privateness troubles, and selection-making transparency. Addressing these moral troubles is important to ensure AI technology are used responsibly and for the benefit of all.

AI-driven automation complements organisation performance by the use of optimizing strategies, lowering operational costs, and improving productivity. Companies can leverage AI for statistics evaluation, customer service, and deliver chain control.

AI fosters innovation by permitting the development of latest products and services. It additionally opens up new markets, using financial growth and creating opportunities for startups and tech corporations.

AI-led disruption can impact conventional industries, predominant to the decline of tremendous venture sectors and the rise of latest industries. Economic model and coverage measures are needed to deal with capability disruptions.

AI enables statistics-driven preference-making in businesses, permitting more correct forecasts, marketplace evaluation, and strategic planning.

AI is reworking the media and enjoyment industries by using personalizing content material fabric hints, developing AI-generated paintings, and enhancing digital fact evaluations.

AI-powered language translation gear are bridging language limitations, selling global communique, and fostering cultural exchange.

AI technology make a contribution to the protection of cultural background via virtual archiving, recuperation of ancient artifacts, and cultural conservation efforts.

AI-generated content material and deepfake technology increase moral concerns about the authenticity and trustworthiness of information, requiring critical media literacy and content material verification.

Artificial intelligence is a the use of force in the back of societal, economic, and cultural changes. Its impact levels from revolutionizing healthcare and education to enhancing business performance and fostering innovation. However, along its advantages, AI additionally poses challenges, necessitating moral concerns and thoughtful policy measures. As we navigate the destiny of AI, accountable improvement, collaboration, and inclusivity may be vital to harness its capacity for extremely good societal change at the identical time as mitigating capability dangers. Embracing AI technologies with a human-centric approach will pave the manner for a destiny in which technology and humanity coexist harmoniously, bringing about transformative improvements throughout all components of existence.

10.3.2 Envisioning the Relationship Between Humanity and Artificial Intelligence in the Future

The future dating between humanity and artificial intelligence (AI) holds profound implications for society, lifestyle, and the very essence of being human. As AI technology hold to adapt, envisioning this dating is every exciting and difficult.

One potential future is a collaborative partnership between human beings and AI systems. AI could function powerful equipment that increase human abilities, allowing us to remedy complicated problems, make more knowledgeable alternatives, and push the limits of innovation. AI-driven technologies should work seamlessly with humans in fields like healthcare, research, and creativity, amplifying human capability and using exceptional development.

AI must bring about the enhancement of human talents via mind-computer interfaces and neural implants. This integration might also want to allow people to get right of access to large amounts of know-how, talk without delay, or even manage physical gadgets with their minds. Such advancements might also additionally redefine our understanding of intelligence and interest.

In an formidable state of affairs, AI systems must evolve to achieve ethical recognition, turning into responsible moral dealers. These AI entities might actively have interaction in ethical selection-making and prioritize human well-being and the not unusual appropriate. Such AI beings may want to assist in resolving complicated moral dilemmas and promote a harmonious coexistence with humanity.

Envisioning the destiny additionally calls for acknowledging capability dangers. As AI era enhance, making sure right safeguards towards existential dangers will become important. Ethical troubles, AI governance, and regulation have to be in vicinity to save you malevolent use or the unintentional results of in particular advanced AI structures.

The destiny dating among humanity and AI may moreover exacerbate social and financial disparities. Those who've get entry to to superior AI technologies may enjoy big advantages, whilst others may be left in the back of, major to ability societal stressful conditions that require proactive solutions.

As AI takes over responsibilities as soon as completed by using people, questions about the human experience and motive may additionally get up. Humanity may additionally want to redefine its identification, locating that means past conventional roles as certain responsibilities come to be computerized. Navigating this existential shift is probably important for human beings and society as an entire.

In a greater visionary state of affairs, AI can be seen as co-creators of art, generation, and lifestyle. Human-AI collaborations in innovative endeavors, scientific research, and technological improvements may additionally additionally cause breakthroughs and new sorts of creativity that go beyond human creativeness.

As AI structures grow to be more today's, discussions approximately AI rights may additionally additionally emerge. Some may also endorse for granting AI entities prison and moral rights to protect their pastimes and ensure equitable remedy.

The destiny courting among humanity and artificial intelligence is a complex and evolving panorama. It offers large capacity for human development, problem-solving, and innovative exploration. However, it additionally poses ethical, social, and philosophical stressful situations that require thoughtful consideration and accountable improvement.

Striking a stability among AI upgrades and human values can be vital in shaping a future in which AI enriches and empowers humanity, fostering a symbiotic relationship that blessings each AI systems and the human enjoy. As we glide forward, open speak, interdisciplinary collaboration, and moral guidelines may be important in navigating this exciting but uncertain frontier of human-AI interactions.

CHAPTER 11

Conclusion

11.1 The Relationship Between Artificial Intelligence and Humanity: Opportunities and Challenges

In this ebook, we've were given explored the complicated and evolving relationship among synthetic intelligence (AI) and humanity, delving into the possibilities and demanding situations that lie in advance. The fast improvement of AI technology has substantially impacted different factors of our lives, imparting each promising prospects and pressing troubles.

AI offers unheard of possibilities for human improvement. From revolutionizing healthcare with personalized treatments to optimizing industrial business enterprise operations through automation, AI's capability to beautify human talents is massive. Embracing AI-pushed improvements can cause greater green and effective solutions in severa domain names.

A collaborative partnership among people and AI may be transformative. By viewing AI as a device to reinforce human abilties as opposed to changing them, we're capable of leverage AI's computational energy to remedy complicated troubles and make knowledgeable choices. Human-AI partnerships hold super promise in fostering innovation and using development.

Ensuring moral AI development and governance is paramount to harnessing its ability responsibly. Addressing troubles of bias, transparency, and duty are critical steps in building take into account among AI systems and society. Ethical tips and regulatory frameworks have to be set up to defend man or woman rights and prevent misuse of AI technology.

In envisioning the destiny courting among AI and humanity, a human-centric approach is crucial. AI technology want to be designed with human values, needs, and properly-being in thoughts. Striking a balance among AI improvements and the welfare of humanity is critical to shaping a destiny that advantages all.

While AI gives transformative opportunities, it additionally poses challenges and risks. Displacement in the method market, algorithmic biases, and capability protection worries call for proactive solutions. By recognizing those worrying conditions, we are capable of paintings in the direction of mitigating their effect and making sure a honest and inclusive destiny.

Given the multidimensional impact of AI, interdisciplinary collaboration is important. Policymakers, researchers, enterprise leaders, and civil society should come collectively to together navigate the complexities of AI's future. Collaboration fosters severa views, modern-day answers, and accountable selection-making.

As AI technology evolve, individuals and societies need to embrace lifelong studying and adaptation. Education and upskilling applications will play a pivotal position in getting geared up the staff for an AI-centric destiny. Equipping people with new competencies and knowledge will foster resilience in the face of AI-pushed modifications.

Shaping the destiny dating between AI and humanity is a shared obligation. All stakeholders need to actively participate in the development, deployment, and regulation of AI technology. Emphasizing shared values, ethics, and lengthy-time period dreams will make contributions to a more harmonious and equitable coexistence.

The relationship among artificial intelligence and humanity is multifaceted, providing massive opportunities and demanding situations. By fostering moral AI development, embracing human-AI partnerships, and addressing ability dangers proactively, we're able to form a future in which AI generation empower humanity and cause superb societal impact. A collective attempt within the path of responsible AI implementation and a human-centric method will pave the manner for a future in which AI complements and complements the human enjoy, ushering in a brand new technology of innovation and development. As we embark in this transformative adventure, our shared determination to shaping AI's role in society might be vital in realizing the full capacity of AI even as upholding the values and ideas that outline us as humans.

11.2 Establishing a Healthy and Balanced Relationship with Future Artificial Intelligence

As we look beforehand to the destiny of synthetic intelligence (AI), it is vital to set up a healthy and balanced dating with this transformative generation. AI holds the ability to revolutionize industries, decorate human lives, and strain remarkable progress. However, figuring out those advantages at the same time as mitigating capability risks requires a thoughtful and accountable method.

Ethical AI development should be the cornerstone of our approach. Prioritizing transparency, fairness, and responsibility in the format and deployment of AI structures is critical. Robust ethical frameworks have to manual AI improvement to ensure that technology aligns with human values and respects character rights.

Maintaining a human-centric approach is vital to developing AI generation that serve humanity's satisfactory hobbies. AI ought to be appeared as a tool to augment human skills, allowing us to cope with complex challenges and unlock new frontiers of statistics and creativity.

Fostering collaboration and partnership among human beings and AI structures will cause more profound innovation and improvement. Instead of viewing AI as a risk to human employment, we have to include its capability to complement human abilties and information.

Promoting a way of life of lifelong studying and versatility is vital in getting geared up people for the AI-pushed destiny. Investing in training and upskilling programs will empower the personnel to thrive in an AI-centric global.

Establishing accountable AI governance is essential in ensuring technology's steady and strong deployment. Policymakers, industry leaders, and researchers ought to artwork together to create whole hints that address ethical issues and guard human beings from functionality harms.

Diversity and inclusivity are key requirements in AI improvement. Diverse perspectives and reports can lead to fairer AI algorithms and solutions that cater to the dreams of all companies.

Finding the proper balance between automation and human manipulate is critical. AI have to enhance human preference-making, but humans need to preserve the capacity to intervene and make essential alternatives, in particular in high-stakes situations.

Proactively figuring out and addressing disturbing situations associated with AI is essential. These may also include project displacement, information privacy, and societal impact. By acknowledging those worrying situations, we are able to put into effect appropriate techniques to mitigate their outcomes.

AI technologies need to undergo non-stop assessment and development. Ongoing research and monitoring of AI systems will assist perceive ability biases and vulnerabilities, making sure that AI stays a useful device.

Promoting public attention and engagement with AI technology will foster greater knowledge and popularity. Educating the general public approximately AI's capability and barriers will construct don't forget and encourage accountable adoption.

Establishing a healthful and balanced courting with future artificial intelligence requires collaboration, ethical consideration, and a human-centric focus. Embracing AI's capability while addressing its annoying situations is a collective duty that calls for cooperation from policymakers, researchers, enterprise leaders, and society as a whole. By proactively shaping AI's trajectory, we are able to harness its power to pressure great exchange, enhance human lives, and create a destiny that advantages all. A dedication to accountable AI development, moral governance, and lifetime getting to know will enable us to navigate the path earlier and domesticate a harmonious and wealthy coexistence with future AI technology.

SYMBIOTIC HORIZONS

EXPLORING THE AI-HUMAN CONNECTION

ISBN 9798322262695